FROM

A SCOURGE OF HYACINTHS

'Unquestionably Africa's most versatile writer and arguably one of her finest.'
New York Times Book Review

When the Military decrees that a crime carrying a prison sentence now retroactively warrants summary execution, confusion and fear permeate a society where the brutality and injustice of military rule is parodied by life inside prison.

Wole Soyinka was born in Nigeria in 1934. Educated there and at Leeds University, he worked in the British theatre before returning to West Africa in 1960, where he has since been based. In 1986 he became the first African writer to win the Nobel Prize for Literature. His plays include *The Jero Plays* (1960, 1966), *The Road* (1965), *The Lion and the Jewel* (1966), *Madmen and Specialists* (1971) and *A Play of Giants* (1984). His novels include *The Interpreters* (1973) and *Season of Anomy* (1980) and his collections of poetry include *Idanre* (1967), *A Shuttle in the Crypt* (1972), a volume of poems written during a period of over two years in prison without trial and *Mandela's Earth* (1990). His autobiographical volumes, *Aké, The Years of Childhood* and *Ìsarà* were published in 1981 and 1989 respectively. His collection of essays, *Art, Dialogue and Outrage* was published in 1988.

Wole Soyinka

FROM ZIA, WITH LOVE
and
A SCOURGE OF HYACINTHS

METHUEN DRAMA

A METHUEN MODERN PLAY

First published in Great Britain in 1992
by Methuen Drama, Michelin House,
81 Fulham Road, London sw3 6rb

From Zia, With Love copyright © 1992
by Wole Soyinka
A Scourge of Hyacinths copyright © 1992
by Wole Soyinka

The author has asserted his moral rights

isbn 0–413–67240–9

A CIP catalogue record for this book is available
from the British Library

*The photograph of the author on the back cover is by
Ulf Karlsson (Associated Press)*

Phototypeset by Wilmaset Limited, Wirral
Printed and bound in Great Britain by
Cox & Wyman Ltd, Reading, Berkshire

Caution

FROM ZIA, WITH LOVE

Based on an actual event which took place in Nigeria, in 1984, under the Military rule of generals Buhari and Idiagbon, this play is however an entire product of the imagination, and makes no claim whatever to any correlation with actuality.

From Zia, With Love was premièred in Sienna, Italy in
June 1992, with the following cast:

HYACINTH	Richard Mofe-Damijo
ADC, SERGEANT, *etc*	Victor Onyiliagha
DIRECTOR OF SECURITY	Yomi Obileye
MINISTER OF INFORMATION AND CULTURE	
EDUCATION	Tunji Oleyana
WATER	Yewande Johnson
AGRICULTURE	Femi Fatoba
HEALTH	Lanre Durodola
LABOUR	
HOME AFFAIRS	
WING COMMANDER	Yomi Obileye
NUMBER 2	Wale Ogunyemi/ Femi Fatoba
SEBE	Femi Fatoba/ Tunji Oyelana
STUDENT	Segun Sofowote
MIGUEL DOMINGO	Bankole Olayebi
DETIBA	Fatai Adiyeloja
EMUKE	Wale Ogunyemi
WOMAN SUPPLIANT	Yewande Johnson
SUPERINTENDENT	Ibidun Allison
AREMU/WARDER	Durodola Olanrewaju
FIRST TRUSTY	Yewande Johnson
SECOND TRUSTY	Tunji Oyelana
THIRD TRUSTY	Segun Sofowote
LOUDSPEAKER VOICE	Segun Sofowote
SICK MAN/PRISONER	Bisi Toluwase/ Arthur Aginam
PASSER-BY	Promise Onwudiwe

A row of cells in a half-arc on one side of the stage. On the other side is one large cell, lit by a kerosene lantern and two or three candles. A burly, scar-faced figure sits on a plastic chair which is mounted on packing cases. He is the cell COMMANDANT. *His conduct is slightly manic. A Naval Officer cap is perched jauntily on his head. Behind him stands another inmate 'shouldering arms' with a broomstick, while another stands at the entrance with a piece of plank held like a sub-machine gun. The inmates are a mixed bag — first offenders and hardened convicts, political detainees, 'awaiting-trial', etc. They include some disabled, semi-crazed or eccentric as well as the restless and listless. In a corner is a large metal dustbin which serves the inmates as a latrine. Suspicious stains are clearly visible on the floor and on the walls around the bin; that corner of the floor is also wet. The odd rags, worn towels, enamel and tin mugs and plates, etc. complete the accessories. Against the cell bars hangs a crude board with the sign; 'Abandon Shame All Who Enter Here'.*

A human shape is stretched out on a mat next to the cell door. He coughs and shivers from time to time. A small furtive and obsequious type fusses around with some notepaper and bits of newspapers. He is ADC *to the* COMMANDANT. *In the corner with the bucket,* MIGUEL DOMINGO, DETIBA *and* EMUKE *squat on their haunches, obviously trying to avoid the floor. They stick out from the others. Packing cases, broken stools, chairs, benches, camp beds, pillows, buckets, etc. are used deftly to create sets for the various enactments. The 'Cabinet' is in session.*

COMMANDANT. Minister of Health!

HEALTH (*leaps up, salutes briskly*). Present sah!

COMMANDANT. Make your report.

HEALTH. Seven dead sah!

COMMANDANT. Seven dead? You mean between yesterday and today?

HEALTH. In the last twenty-four hours, Your Excellency.

COMMANDANT. Which Local Government?

HEALTH. Katanga Local Government, two; Aburi, one; Soweto, two. And another two in your own constituency, Amorako. Total, seven sir. By tomorrow morning, probably eight (*Pointing in the direction of the tossing figure on the mat*.) At my recommendation, the Minister of Housing has relocated him to maximum fresh-air security by the door, but I think it's too – late. Unless they take him to hospital.

COMMANDANT. So, we have epidemic.

HEALTH. Permission to speak sah.

COMMANDANT. Permission granted.

HEALTH. Your Excellency, yes sir, we have epidemic.

COMMANDANT. Like last year, no?

HEALTH. Like last year, yessah! Started dead on time, with the first rains.

COMMANDANT. In short, the Health situation is stable.

HEALTH. Like a model patient sah, condition critical but stable.

COMMANDANT. Without stability, there can be no development.

NUMBER 2. Well said my Commander. Without stability, there can be no progress.

COMMANDANT. Good. Let's make progress, Security?

ADC. Director of Security Major Awam, by State Command, will once again present his curriculum vitae.

General movement as they all shift to pre-assigned places.

DIRECTOR. Situation report is ready, Commandant sir.

COMMANDANT. Before you begin, let me ask you, are you going to annoy me today?

DIRECTOR. Annoy you sir? Certainly not.

COMMANDANT. Because I warn you, if you do . . .

NUMBER 2. He's assured me he has totally reformed.

COMMANDANT. We'll soon find out. I have yet to hear of the leopard changing his spots.

HEALTH. Let's give him a chance, Your Excellency.

COMMANDANT. All right, proceed. But remember I have my eyes on you!

DIRECTOR (*opens imaginary file, clears his throat*). The natives are restless, sir.

COMMANDANT. I'd be disappointed if they weren't. What next?

DIRECTOR. Sir . . .

COMMANDANT. No! I said, next item. Your job is to take care of restlessness, not bother us with the whys. Move on, Major!

DIRECTOR. Yes sir. Next item is, the religious question.

Audible gasp from one or two. Then silence. The COMMANDANT *sucks in air, expels it, fixes the* DIRECTOR *with a stare.*

COMMANDANT. Major Awam!

DIRECTOR. Yessir.

COMMANDANT. I thought you heard me say . . .

DIRECTOR. It is the next item sir.

COMMANDANT. Don't play your university games with me Major! (*Turning right and left to the others*.) You see? What did I warn you all about? Having university graduates in the army is bad enough, putting them on the Ruling Council . . .

NUMBER 2 (*mildly*). We've been through all that Chief. He

is the only senior officer from that part of the country. It's our luck with the geography.

COMMANDANT. The military should have no geography.

NUMBER 2. In an ideal world yes, but – see what a nation we inherited.

COMMANDANT (*gives the* DIRECTOR *a baleful look*). Then we must change his portfolio.

NUMBER 2. Come on Chief, you know he's good. Look at the way he handled the last student riots.

COMMANDANT. Nothing to boast about. He is just another of them after all. He even thinks like a student.

DIRECTOR. But sir, you commended my handling of the workers' demonstration.

COMMANDANT. Yes yes yes, and you don't let us forget it. Maybe you should change Ministries with Danlako. You handle Labour and let him switch to Security.

LABOUR. No no Chief. I'd rather return to the barracks.

COMMANDANT. We'll have to do some reshuffling before long. Or split Security in two. Even three. I'll leave him Military Intelligence and get someone else for National Security. All right, proceed Major. Go straight to the next item.

DIRECTOR. Yes sir. Item Three; food shortage.

COMMANDANT. What about food shortage? Have you taken over the Agriculture portfolio?

DIRECTOR. No sir.

AGRICULTURE. I should hope not indeed!

Guffaws from the Cabinet.

DIRECTOR. Do I have permission to move on sir?

COMMANDANT. Permission granted.

DIRECTOR. The hyacinths are still a hazard to navigation.

COMMANDANT. That's why everybody calls me Hyacinth, so what?

Dutiful laugh from Cabinet.

DIRECTOR. The fishermen can't get at the fish . . .

WATER (*protesting*). My portfolio sir – Water Resources.

AGRICULTURE. No, mine. Agriculture.

COMMANDANT. Silence! Any more of that ancient bickering and I'll merge both Ministries into Agriculture and Water Resources then abolish both in one stroke instead of two! While you are arguing, this – this busybody is trespassing on your domain yet again. Yes Major, what were you saying? Do carry on. Annoy me.

DIRECTOR. Soon there'll be a serious protein shortage . . .

HEALTH. Health, health, Major Awam. Keep your paddles out of the stream of Health – if you want to stay healthy.

DIRECTOR. If we lose the fishing it means there'll be a shortage from that food resource. Add that to what the Kwela birds have done to the grain crops this year, and anyone can predict that . . .

CABINET (*derisive chorus*). . . . We are clearly heading for food shortage!

DIRECTOR (*unflapped*). And possible food riots.

COMMANDANT. Have you landed?

DIRECTOR. On this item, yes, Commandant sir!

COMMANDANT. Good. Now let me tell you what you've left out. Would you like to know?

DIRECTOR. Yes, Commandant.

COMMANDANT. You left out what should interest your portfolio – Security. While you were drifting from portfolio to portfolio, minding other people's departments, you missed your boat. And that boat is – Security. With the water hyacinths spreading through the harbours, the nation cannot be invaded by sea. You can't have any secret landings on unguarded beaches. Those sea-borne mercenary and guerilla incursions have ceased – that is Security for you. Even our waterside prisons have become more secure – Ita Oko Penal island for instance – there has been no escape from there in the past year and a half – that is security, your portfolio. Cheap, natural, security barrier, what more can you ask for? Gentlemen, I propose three hearty cheers for the water hyacinths – Hip! Hip! Hip!

INMATES. Hurray!

COMMANDANT. Hip! Hip! Hip!

INMATES. Hurray!

COMMANDANT (*standing*). And make this a truly big one for Commodore Hyacinth himself, the Commander-in-Chief, and your Cell Commandant – Hip! Hip! Hip!

INMATES (*throwing buckets, cups, brooms, etc. in air*). Hurray-ay-ay-ay-ay!!!

COMMANDANT (*waves his arms grandly*). Now that is the sound of stability. And Security. (*Sits*.) Proceed Major, and no more clever-clever circumnavigations or poaching in other people's ponds and fishing in troubled waters. Give us a professional Sit-Rep. (*Looks round*.) Sit-Rep. Situation Report, for you bloody civilians.

DIRECTOR. Thank you, sir. Item Four: Public Transportation.

COMMANDANT (*throws up his arms and rolls his eyes*). Public Transportation. Did I hear the Major say Public Transportation?

DIRECTOR. Yessir. Public Transportation.

COMMANDANT. Major Awam, I know this is only your second session with the new Eternal Ruling Council, but . . .

NUMBER 2. Please sir, let me. Look here Awam, all this

should have become clear to you by now. Across this chamber is the Minister of Transportation. He speaks to Public Transportation. Mass Transit, Water Transport, the National Railway, Airways etc., etc. Your territory is National Security. You are embarrassing me, considering how I have just vouched for you.

DIRECTOR. Sir, I *am* speaking on the subject of National Security.

COMMANDANT. See? Will you please tell us what National Security has to do with Public Transportation? Or food supply? Or . . . what else, what else? What were the other fields you've tried to appropriate in the last few minutes? You began with religion I think. Well, maybe you'll excuse yourself there because we don't have a Ministry of Religious Affairs. That last Aafa we had was hanged for ritual murder and we've had no replacement. But we do have a Minister for Transportation, Major! Leave him to address his own portfolio.

DIRECTOR. Sir, intelligence reports . . . the potential flash points – have you seen those long queues after work, in the broiling sun? And especially now we've lost the use of the ferries, thanks to . . .

COMMANDANT. Ferries! Transportation! Potential flash points! See, grammar! Nothing but grammar. No, wait, it's worse. He's done it again. I tell you, he's done it again. He's circled back to Health portfolio.

DIRECTOR. Health sir? I'm not sure I understand.

COMMANDANT. Hot sun. Yes, you said they queue in the broiling sun after work. Are you a brain surgeon that you suggest their brains are likely to explode?

DIRECTOR. Well sir, something is likely to explode.

COMMANDANT. And I am even more likely to explode before any of them, Major. Indeed, I think I will now explode! Right this moment!

Cries of alarm pleas. NUMBER 2 *calms down the* COMMANDANT *and turns to the* DIRECTOR.

NUMBER 2. My dear young Major, your problem is lack of experience. You must forget all your funny ideas in here, you understand? On this council, security means only one thing — counter-subversion, counter-subversive talk. Counter rumour-mongering. Counter incitement to subversion. And you have been given powers to deal with all that. Am I right so far?

DIRECTOR. Quite correct sir.

NUMBER 2. There is no potential flash point in your mandate, Major, except this one you create by encroaching on the portfolio of the Minister of Transport. Or Health. Kindly limit yourself to matters of national security.

DIRECTOR. Yessir, yessir. That will be all sir.

Astonished looks are exchanged round the Cabinet.

COMMANDANT. All? What do you mean that will be all?

DIRECTOR. I mean, that's the end of the security report sir.

COMMANDANT. Are you trying to tell me that is the full security report you have brought before this council?

DIRECTOR. Yesssir.

NUMBER 2 (*restraining the* COMMANDANT *as he is about to 'explode'*). Major Awam, what the Commander-in-Chief is trying to say is — where, for example, is the list of the new detainees? How many organisations have you identified as fronts for subversive activities? And so on and so forth. We like to know what's going on in your department. The stability of the nation requires that the council be kept up to date in these matters.

DIRECTOR. List, sir? I have no list. There are no new detainees.

Silence: exaggerated stares of horror are exchanged.

HOME. Let me get this right, Major Awam. Are you saying that you have not detained anyone since you took over the Department of National Security?

DIRECTOR. Just that, sir.

HOME. You have disbanded your team of agents?

DIRECTOR. No sir. I have dismissed some and recruited others – a different calibre altogether. The overall strength remains the same. I think we have a more accurate feel of the national pulse as a result.

HOME. Maybe you have dismantled your listening posts?

DIRECTOR. Not exactly sir. But they are now diversified. More flexible than before.

NUMBER 2. Then perhaps the Information Fund has run dry? You need a new subvention?

DIRECTOR. On the contrary sir, we now disburse only about half from that fund. But the results remain . . .

COMMANDANT (*exploding*). Unreliable Major, unreliable! As proved by your lack of information. Informers must be paid or they do not inform. And where there is no information, there cannot be detainees.

DIRECTOR. With all due respects sir, my assessment of the situation is that we should begin to consider the cases of those presently in detention. The intelligence I have received is that most of them need not be there a day longer.

COMMANDANT. Quiet Director, I have heard enough. I think the entire Council has had enough. Those thieving politicians from whom we saved this nation – is it the heartless prodigals you now propose we should release from detention?

DIRECTOR. If I may sir . . .

COMMANDANT (*increasingly violent. Half-way through, he has risen from his seat*). Or the radicals? Those extremists who open their stinking mouths to demand of us a date for restoration of civil rule? Democracy! Democracy! We have hardly begun our mission of redemption. Where were the bleeding hearts when the nation was being plundered with such unprecedented abandon? Where was their patriotism? Their human rights conscience? Did the very people on whose behalf they now claim to speak – did not those very masses pour out into the streets to celebrate our takeover of government? Who are they to open their mouths now to demand a swift return to civil rule? Just tell us Major, do such people speak for this nation? Or is it the army which has the moral right to speak and act on behalf of the masses? What do they want anyway? Eunuchs! Impotents! Incompetents! Agitators! What the hell do they want? None of us has earned promotion. We have retained our original ranks since we staged this eternal revolution. I could have made myself Admiral both Rear and Front but I remain simple Commodore and Commander-in-Chief. Compare it to the damned universities where they have six professors per department and in some cases there is no teaching because they're all professors and professors only profess, they do not teach. Oh yes Mr Director you are a fifth columnist in our midst you have been planted here by those bearded bastards and you have been tempting me to explode and geographical spread and quota or no quota I think I am just about ready to explode!

CHORUS. Explode!

COMMANDANT. Shall I explode?

CHORUS. Explode!

COMMANDANT. Am I or am I not overdue for explosion?

A loud explosion follows effected by the SERGEANT-MAJOR *with an inflated paper bag.* COMMANDANT *sinks back in his chair, exhausted. Applause from the* INMATES.

DIRECTOR. Thank you comrades, thank you. And thank you especially, Cell Commandant and Commander-in-Chief of Amaroko for so competently assisting me in the thirty-seventh presentation of my curriculum vitae.

COMMANDANT. My pleasure, my pleasure. My master, the late Maestro Hubert Ogunde himself must be looking down on me from his heavenly abode and applauding with his usual energy.

NUMBER 2. Commandant, I hope he won't discover from which kind of stage you are giving us this performance.

COMMANDANT. Of course he must. He was in and out of prison himself a few times. I am only following in his footsteps.

CHORUS (*groans and moans of disagreement*). 'Oga sah, I beg, no to same thing o.' 'In own different.' 'Baba no dey carry cocaine o.' 'Ogunde na political prisoner.' etc., etc.

COMMANDANT. Shurrup! Shurrup! Prison na prison. (*Pointing rapidly round.*) Political detainee dey here. Manslaughter dey. (*Points upwards.*) Innocents dey over yonder (*points to the cell.*) Mistake dey here. Even coup plotter, e dey here, abi I lie, Mr Director?

DIRECTOR. Suspicions. Mere suspicions. I'm just a talker, I enjoy a bit of agitating over matters I really care about. That's all. But they got nervous and decided to get rid of me. You can see how long they've kept me here without trial. The ones who don't talk – they're the ones to look out for. Me, I don't plot coups. I believe in the power of truth.

The COMMANDANT's *expression changes abruptly.*

COMMANDANT. Fe-e-e-e-em!

Instant silence. The COMMANDANT *regains his authoritative posture.*

I'll have to watch out for you Major. See? He believes in the power of truth. No wonder he's here. Major, you are a security risk. A spoilsport. Your CV was most entertaining but – look around. Look at all the faces.

All heads are instantly dropped.

You have depressed everyone. I decree a change of mood.

He is applauded.

COMMANDANT (*makes a move of looking over the agenda*). Call the Minister for Home Affairs.
ADC. Honourable Minister for Home Affairs!
HOME (*rises briskly and salutes*). – Aye aye sir.
COMMANDANT. Make your report.
HOME. Reporting three new refugees delivered to Amaroko Local Government this afternoon, sir. No notice. I have taken the liberty to allocate them accommodation in the transit quarters.

All eyes turn to the three men squatting near the latrine bucket.

COMMANDANT. I see. Are they present and correct?
HOME. All present and correct, sir.
ADC. Sergeant-Major!

SERGEANT-MAJOR *throws a brisk salute then yanks up* DETIBA *who is nearest to him and catapults him towards the podium.* MIGUEL DOMINGO *receives the same treatment while* EMUKE, *taking his cue from the others, leaps up and dashes in their direction. The* COMMANDANT *gives a prolonged stare at the two figures scrambling to their feet and at* EMUKE *who is standing apprehensively, casting desperate looks around him. The* INMATES *watch dispassionately.*

COMMANDANT. Welcoming committee, step forward.

Flanked by two others, the SERGEANT-MAJOR *strides forward, positions himself behind the group.*

Introduce them to our local government.

A barrage of slaps descend on the men, right and left. They are eventually beaten to their knees.

COMMANDANT (*signals when he thinks they have had enough. Points to* MIGUEL). Beginning with you, give us your curriculum vitae.

MIGUEL. I don't understand. What have we done?

Another slap descends from behind.

SERGEANT-MAJOR. You don't understand, what?

MIGUEL. Please, please, just tell us if we have done something wrong. Why are you attacking us like this? We only came in this afternoon.

SERGEANT-MAJOR. You said, when talking to the Commodore, Commandant and Commander-in-Chief 'I don't understand', I then gave you a chance to correct yourself. Now, try again – You don't understand – what?

MIGUEL *is confused. Looks round the cell for help.*

COMMANDANT (*leans forward. Accommodating manner*). You are uneducated, that is your problem. I will help you, but it will cost.

MIGUEL. Anything, anything you want.

COMMANDANT. You look like a man of resources. And influence. Very likely you will even be taken to a different local government. The doctor will likely prescribe you special diet – bread, omelette, beans with no worms, soft toilet paper, ovaltine, milk, sugar, fresh fish on Fridays, jollof rice with chicken stew on Sundays . . .

PRISONERS (*writhing, salivating noisily*). – Mum-m-m-m, nm-mm. . . . Na so, na so.

COMMANDANT. So I will treat you like a man of substance. A man of enviable potential. Even like a tycoon but, lacking education. No culture.

MIGUEL. Thank you, thank you very much.

SERGEANT-MAJOR (*raises his arm again to strike*). Thank you very much – what?

COMMANDANT (*signals restraint*). No, no, he is to be assisted, he and his two friends. And of course he will pay. Won't you, gentlemen?

MIGUEL. Of course. I swear. I have means.

COMMANDANT. Hn-hn. Don't try and be like one businessman politician we once welcomed here. After he transferred to his special hostel he forgot us. In fact, he went and reported us to the prison authorities.

Breaks into a prolonged guffaw which is taken up by the INMATES. *Cuts it off with another gesture.*

Well, he learnt his lesson. That became double education. And he had to pay for that new education from the military hospital where he was sent to recover. And paid for the first also, with interest. So, don't try and disgrace yourself. I am vouching for you personally, on my own personal authority. You understand?

MIGUEL *nods. So do the other two.*

Good. I think now we can say that we understand each other. Minister of Education!

EDUCATION. Yes, Commandant.

COMMANDANT. Educate these refugees.

EDUCATION. Yes, sir, Commodore and Commander-in-Chief. (*Turns to the kneeling men.*) Now you! You had your ears open just now. I hope you heard me when I addressed the Commander-in-Chief. Right? What the Sergeant-Major was complaining about was that you addressed our Commander like a common man. When you address the Commodore, you say 'Sir'. Is that clear?

MIGUEL/DETIBA/EMUKE. Oh yes, thank you. We're very sorry sir.

EDUCATION. Yesssir. No, sir. I beg your pardon, sir. I understand, sir. Permission to speak, sir. Permission to fall out, sir. And so on and so forth. This is a military regime so don't mess about. Even when we were doing the civilian style – because you see, we try to conform with what is going on in the country outside – so before we changed to military, even then our Commandant was still Commander-in-Chief as well as civilian President. So, no matter what style we are operating, you must address him with due respect and full protocol.

MIGUEL. Yessir. (*Turning to the* COMMANDANT.) I apologise, sir.

COMMANDANT *graciously gestures that all is forgiven.*

EDUCATION. Now, your curriculum vitae – I think an educated man like yourself should know what that means.

I am very disappointed and shocked that you can be
ignorant on such a simple matter. It means also that you
were not paying much attention to what went on just now.

MIGUEL. I'm sorry, sir. I know what it means outside . . .

EDUCATION. Outside or inside, the same thing. You
think we don't follow procedure here? Name. Age. Profession. And then, most important of all, wetin bring you
here? What crime you commit? How much sentence they
give you? If you don't give us your full record, how can the
Eternal Ruling Council plan the economy or make the
Five-Year Revolving Development Plan?

MIGUEL. True sir, you are quite right.

COMMANDANT. Minister for Information and Culture,
take over.

INFORMATION (*steps forward*). Yes, Commandant, sir.
Now you, in presenting your curriculum vitae, you can
turn it into 'ewi' for us and recite it, or you can sing and
dance it – anything – juju, talazo, fuji or disco style – we
don't mind. Or you can preach it like a sermon, in which
case you can repeat it any Friday or Sunday, depending on
which religion you follow. And last but not the least, as
you saw just now, you can play it for us. Only, that will
take time to prepare. But we are all here to help – you will
pay fees to all those you recruit. The play is our favourite
of course, especially for the Commodore. He was trained
by the late Hubert Ogunde himself, but that was many
many years ago.

COMMANDANT. I am still expert, mind you. (*Sharply.*)
And I take the first pick of the roles. And more than one if
I like. I'm a Master of Disguise.

MIGUEL. Of course sir, I understand.

COMMANDANT. You can depend on me. I learn my parts
very quickly. It came in useful in one of my many lines of
business. I am very versatile you see.

INMATES (*they chant*). Oga Versatility – Versati. Oga
Versatility-Versati. Oga Versatility . . .

COMMANDANT. Don't mind them. They are just jealous
of my talents. Ask the Police – when they booked me for
my very first impersonation, over thirty years ago, I fooled
them into locking up the genuine person in my stead –
that's how good I was. Anyway, those were small-time
days. Undergraduate times – Shurrup! I know what they
were going to chant. But whether you believe am or not, I
tell you say I go University. (*He looks round fiercely*.)
Education, proceed.

EDUCATION. Yessir Commodore and Commander-in-
Chief. E-eh, yes. I think that's all for your first lesson. But
of course, you will first give us a shorthand account of your
crime. That one is immediate and compulsory. Because
you may be transferred from here tomorrow and then we
would miss your contribution to our Development Plan.
We have to put you on trial, you know. The sentence you
get outside, that is their own. In here, we must pass our
own judgement, and sentence you.

COMMANDANT. Enough. That is already lessons one
and two. Now, you have met the Minister of Education
and the Minister of Information and Culture. Between the
two of them, they will inform you about all our tradition
and customs in this local government. You must learn
everybody's rank, because if you make a mistake . . .
Look, why don't I simply introduce you to everybody.
Would you like that? Get to know your fellow citizens.

MIGUEL. Yessir, that would be kind of you.

COMMANDANT. Good, good. (*Looks round in surprise*.)
Look at them, look at them! I say I want to introduce
everybody and look at them still standing and sitting all
over the place.

SERGEANT-MAJOR (*jumping to action*). Line up, line

up! Line up in alphabetical order. (*Shoves and harries them into what is obviously a familiar formation.*)

COMMANDANT (*preening*). We run a democracy here you see, so everything is done by alphabetical order. We begin with 'A', so I come first. May I welcome you formally – Commodore 'Ayacinth at your service.

INMATES *salute him with the ode to* COMMODORE HYACINTH. *A 'parade-ground dance' accompanies the chorus, while they mark time.*

INMATES.
Behold the lilies of the field.
They do not toil, or sow or build

    Oh hail the Commander
    Rear-Admiral Hyacinth
    Cool as salamander
    Rigid as a plinth

Ours are the lilies of murky waters
Unsinkable flotsam of rancid gutters

    Legend in their own time
    Legend out of time
    Legend in no time at all
    Overland or maritime

Their roots have dug to bed and sludge
What sprat shall tell the whale to budge?

    Oh hail the Commander, etc.

Oh what a paradox they pose
Rootless, yet they've spread huge toes

    Legend in their own time, etc.

Vast as the kapok's buttress roots
Fretting and squirming in camouflage boots

   Oh hail the Commander, etc.

Bloated from the anorexic flea
To vampire bats on the elephant's ear

   Legend in their own time etc.

'Well, is it edible?' queried the nutritionist
'No harm in a trial,' offered the abortionist

   Oh hail the Commander, etc.

Sour as the taste of the morning after
A brothel's night of booze and laughter

   Legend in their own time, etc.

Stubbornly green as the bilious memory
You try in vain to cremate or to bury

   Oh hail the Commander, etc.

A godsend, crowed fibre trade
Here floats free raw material aid

   Legend in their own time, etc.

But that machine was not yet invented
To pulp the weeds for the gains they'd scented

   Oh hail the Commander, etc.

Monster from the sea, was another verdict
Feeds on pollution like a heroin addict

   Legend in their own time, etc.

A mammoth dredger ordered from Soughborough
Heaved and strained and cut a furrow

    Oh hail the Commander, etc.

Too soon, we gave a victory cheer
The weeds had closed up in its rear

    Legend in their own time, etc.

Deadly defoliants, left over from Vietnam
Proved sweet as rain, as dew to a river clam

    Oh hail the Commander, etc.

They split like the Red Sea, immune to fear
Of napalm, conqueror of the ozonisphere

    Legend in their own time, etc.

Then, coolly, respread their death-green coverlet
To drown Mr Napalm with a hiss and a whimperlet

    Oh hail the legend, etc.

Saddam was contacted – prime your chemical fuse
The Green Berets are here, masquerading as lettuce

    Legend in their own time, etc.

No way, said the terror of mighty petroleum
Wait till I've perfected my bomb plutonium

    Oh hail the legend, etc.

Oh hail sweet lilies of our murky grey waters
Midnight guests, eternal squatters
Homely as the gecko, slippery as the eel
Cool as salamander, tempered as steel.

Footsteps are heard approaching. A LOOK-OUT moves closer to the cell door.

LOOK-OUT. Visitors! Scramble!
COMMANDANT (*his gesture commands instant silence*).
Hn, that sounds more than the usual night patrol . . .

A WARDER dashes in the cell door, panicky.

COMMANDANT. What's happening?
WARDER. Scramble! Scramble! The Superintendent himself is here with some people.

Instant activity. The lights are blown out, leaving only the corridor light. Mats and mattresses are rolled back in place and occupied. In a moment there are only audible snores. Enter the SUPERINTENDENT accompanied by two OFFICERS.

SUPERINTENDENT. Open up!

A WARDER unlocks the door.

Order them out.
AREMU. Mr Domingo. Emuke, Detiba.

Answering sounds from the interior.

Pick up your things and come outside.

Grumbling and curses as they stumble over bodies en route.

SUPERINTENDENT. My sincere apologies Mr Domingo, you should never have been brought here. These two occupied a cell already and they should have been returned there, together with you.

As they turn to leave, voices emerge from the cell's interior.

COMMANDANT. Oga, we dey die here o. We done petition so tey we done tire. I tell you say we dey die one by one.

HEALTH. Everybody skin here get craw-craw. The one wey not get craw-craw, 'e get beri-beri. De one wey no get beri-beri, 'e get kwashi-okor. De one wey no get kwashi-okor, 'e get jedi-jedi. De one wey no get jedi-jedi . . .

COMMANDANT (*leaps up and presses his face against the bars*). Oga, I hope you dey listen o. Dat na my Minister of Health. This man wey dey here dey vomit all in belle night and day. Make you come take am for emergency now now or 'e no go last till morning.

WARDER. Oh shut up Hyacinth and get back to sleep.

They proceed offstage.

COMMANDANT. Shurrup yourself you common fuckin-rin warder! You think I dey talk to the like of you. Oga Superintendent na to you a dey make complaint. I tell you dis man dey vomit blood and everything wey dey inside am. If you no carry am go emergency now now 'e no go last all night.

As the steps recede further, he grasps the bars of the cell doors and shakes them violently.

Oga warder! Oga Warder!

He changes the violent shake to a rhythmic one, and is soon joined by the other prisoners who bang cups, plates, sticks and join in the chant.

PRISONERS.
Oga warder, Oga warder!
Oga warder, Oga warder!
Craw-craw warder, oga warder
Sobia warder, oga warder

Jedi-jedi warder, oga warder
Gonorrhoea warder, oga warder
Apollo warder, oga warder
Syphillis warder, oga warder
Leprosy warder, oga warder
Akuse warder, oga warder
Asinwin warder, oga warder
Bad-belle warder, oga warder
Kwashi-Okor warder, oga warder
Epilepsy warder, oga warder
Oga warder o, oga warder
Oga warder o, oga warder
Oga warder o, oga warder . . . (*Etc. etc.*)

Someone begins to stamp to the rhythm. In a few moments the cell is filled with gyrating figures in silhouette, the corridor bulb leaving a pool of light forestage so that the sick man remains visible. He makes a valiant effort to sit up, propping himself on the elbow, a ghost of a grin appearing on his face. As the gyrations reach a crescendo, he collapses suddenly. SERGEANT-MAJOR is the first to notice that something is amiss. He pulls out of the circle, kneels by the mattress, and quickly raises the head. He closes the staring eyes, lays down the head, gently.

One by one the others notice, and the dancing comes to a ragged stop. There is total silence as they stare in the direction of the still figure.

COMMANDANT (*violent scream*). Oga Warder-er-er!
(*Light snaps out.*)

SUPERINTENDENT *and his group re-enter stage, stop at cell 'C', whose door is already wide open. A naked electric bulb hangs from the ceiling. EMUKE and*

DETIBA *enter while* DOMINGO *hesitates, looks back at the* SUPERINTENDENT.

SUPERINTENDENT (*gently*). Yes, you too Mr Domingo. You'll be sharing this cell with your . . . with these two.

DOMINGO *joins the others, walks straight to the sole window and stands with his back to the door, looking out. The door is swung shut.*

SUPERINTENDENT. A warder will be along in the morning with an extra mattress. We are short of beds and other items right now, so you'll have to manage. I don't have to tell you, the prison is overcrowded. But the Military Command and Security send everybody in here as if space is no problem. That's how you got thrown among those others in the first place – I apologise for that mistake by my subordinates. I suppose because we are hemmed in by the lagoon, the regime thinks this is the most secure prison. Well, you two are already at home here, I am sure you will show Mr Domingo the ropes.

Embarrassed silence.

I am sorry about how things turned out for you in court this morning but I hope you didn't take the sentence seriously. This regime wants to put a scare in people, that's all. If there is anything we can do for you – under the circumstances – just summon my immediate assistant. I have instructed him to make you as comfortable as possible. All of you. (*Pause.*) Shall I send you reading material? Or some games? (*Turns to* OFFICER.) Don't we have a spare Scrabble set in the office – the one we confiscated from the political detainees? Yes, they can have that. You could also . . .

Hidden loudspeakers come suddenly to life as a MILITARY VOICE *comes over. The* SUPERINTENDENT *glances instinctively at his watch and, together with the other* OFFICERS, *snaps to attention.* DOMINGO *observes them briefly, turns away.*

MILITARY VOICE. A corrupt nation is a nation without a future. Smuggling is economic sabotage. Smuggling is an unpatriotic act; it is next to treason. Nepotism is a form of corruption. Corruption in all forms has been the bane of our nation. Currency trafficking is economic sabotage; it plays into the hands of foreign powers. It is an act of treason and will be treated as such. So is drug trafficking; the trade of death. Avoid it. Expose any dealers you know. Protect the soul of your fatherland. Make BAI your watchword. Support the Battle against Indiscipline. Enrol in your local brigade. Be the eye of the nation.

As a click signals the end of the broadcast, the SUPERINTENDENT *signals to the* WARDER *who slams home the bolt and locks the door. They exit. There is silence, except for a soft lapping of water and marsh noises.*

MIGUEL (*quietly*). So the water hyacinths have spread also to this part of the lagoon. I suppose I ought to feel at home.

Turns and walks across to the door and shakes it gently.

Oh yes, I know this is yet another prison cell, but it's that court I am not so sure about. The tribunal where the sentence was passed. Was that part of it for real?

DETIBA. Was our treatment by those hard-core criminals real? You'd think all prisoners would stick together!

EMUKE (*after a pause, bitterly*). You know wetin I think? Even God no fit forgive people like you, Mr Domingo!

Some tings dey, wey God no go forgive, and 'e be like your foolishness be one of them.

DETIBA. Emuke, leave the man alone. He took enough punishment among those bastards. Let him have some peace.

EMUKE. No, lef me! I wan' say it one time and then I no go say anything again. When the man turn up for court today, I no believe me eyes. I say to myself, abi dis man dey craze?

DETIBA. Well, I said the same thing, didn't I? But – what happened has happened. We are all in the same boat.

EMUKE. No, we no dey inside de same boat. Even from before, na inside separate boat we dey. And in own boat better pass we own. We dey inside custody, so we no get choice. We must appear before tribunal whether we like am or not. But in own case, 'e get bail. The court grant am bail. He get high connection so they gi'am bail. Then he take in own leg walka inside court – after dey done change decree to capital offence. Dat one, na in I no understand. What kin' sense be dat?

DETIBA. Well, it wasn't you alone. Or myself, to tell the truth. I overheard some reporters – even lawyers – saying the same thing. I don't think I paid much attention to my own case. (*Shrugs*.) I already knew the outcome, there was nothing any lawyer could do for me, unless he could bribe enough members of the tribunal. So I passed the time asking myself, why did he come back?

EMUKE. Unless money done pass reach tribunal hand.

DETIBA. Hn-hn. Hn-hn. Either money, or connection. I thought maybe everything had been fixed for him. But when it came to his turn, and the chairman read out the judgement – 'Miguel Domingo – guilty as charged' – ah, I tell you, I began to wonder.

EMUKE. Me too! Na den fear catch me for yansh. I say to

myself, if elephant self fit get craw-craw, wetin common grass-cutter go get?

MIGUEL (*returns to window*). It beats me. How could one have been so completely without any premonition? I have seen this wall from the outside – I don't know how many times – maybe over a hundred times. We used to go boating from the family house in Akoka – quite often we would take this route. Sometimes we simply came to meet the fishermen in the evenings as they came in with their catch – over there, in that direction. The prisoners here would look out from the windows and wave at us. Sometimes we waved back. At least I did. A child didn't know better. Maybe I even waved to someone standing against these same bars. There was nothing like the water hyacinth then, so the fish market was a regular event. (*Pause.*) In all those pleasure rides, I never thought I would be looking out onto that location from this side. The thought never crossed my mind.

EMUKE. You can talk all the grammar wey you want. I done been say am anyway, grammar people no get sense. Chai! Even God no fit approve dat kin' foolishness. My own condition dey pain me too, I confess. But as I say before, me and Detiba we no get choice. Dem refuse us bail, hold us inside twenty-four hour daily lock-up . . . on top of that, na you make dem go put all of we inside that palava cell. Before you come na here we dey jejely. Big tycoon, na 'in dey bring suffer-suffer for petty criminal.

MIGUEL. I suppose we can't even enjoy that occasional distraction now. The hyacinths must have stopped the motor-boats.

EMUKE (*hisses*). The man wan' pretend say 'e no hear me.

DETIBA (*joining* MIGUEL *at the window*). Oh yes, the boats have stopped. Those weeds have made life miserable

for everyone. You can't imagine how it has affected prison
life, Mr Domingo. Before, the canoes – paddles or
outboard motors – they'd come right up to the walls and
attend to business. Every morning, very early. Prisoners
would lower messages and money, then haul up packages
or whatever they'd arranged. The prison officials knew
about it but they turned a blind eye. It made life easier –
something to look forward to. Those of us facing the
lagoon acted as go-betweens for others on that side. But,
during the ten months we've been here, the weeds finally
gained the upper hand. First they fouled up the propellers, so only boats with paddles could come. Then even
the paddles couldn't fight the weeds. For over three
months now, not one canoe has been able to find its way
anywhere close to the wall.

EMUKE. What about the Ijaw boy wey drown?

DETIBA. Oh yes, that was a horrible day. Can you imagine,
we actually watched someone drown one morning. No
way to help. Just watched his legs get more and more
entangled in those slimy long roots. It was as if some
hidden monster kept dragging him down.

MIGUEL. You saw him?

DETIBA. Everybody watched, everyone on the water side
of the prison. You see, after the boats gave up, he and two,
maybe three other strong swimmers would find a passage
through the hyacinths with waterproof packs and carry on
business. The scale was reduced of course but, it was still
better than this daily nothing. Then the other swimmers
also gave up, leaving only him. Until one Sunday morning . . .

MIGUEL. This window? You watched him through this
window?

EMUKE. Which other window you see inside here?

DETIBA *gestures to* EMUKE *to ease off, and finds a seat closer to him.*

MIGUEL (*softly*). I have never seen death at close quarters, not even on the roads with all their carnage.

EMUKE *brushes off* DETIBA's *mimed efforts at restraint.*

EMUKE. Wetin make you come back, Mister? I wan' know. I no sabbe dat kin' ting at all. Your family get money, dem get property, dem get plenty influence. You fit dey Russia or Australia by now and nobody fit catch up. Wetin happen? I just wan' know. You bribe tribunal and den dey disappoint you? Hen? For my home town, people for say na your enemy take medicine spoil your mind for dat kin' ting to happen.

DETIBA. Let the man have his peace, Emuke. He'll tell us in his own time. After all we'll have plenty of it on our hands. (*Bitter laugh*.) A whole life sentence of it.

EMUKE. That's if they no fire us tomorrow. These soja people, I no trust them. They fit wake up tomorrow and say – line up everybody awaiting execution. Fire them one time!

DETIBA. No-o-o. Even when that Chairman was passing sentence, I had begun to think how many years we would actually spend in gaol. I agree with that Superintendent.

EMUKE. Wetin you dey talk? You no take your own ear hear sentence? Hey, Mr Domingo, wetin you think?

MIGUEL. What?

EMUKE (*irritably*). The man mind done travel! Detiba and I dey argue about this sentence. You think na 'sakara' den dey make? You tink dey no go put us for firing squad?

MIGUEL. I am afraid they won't; yes, that's what I'm

afraid of. Because I can't think of passing twenty years or more behind these walls. Behind any walls. But I fear they will commute it to life. It's obvious.

EMUKE. We go see. All I know is dat dis na wicked country to do something like this. We know some country wey, if you steal they cut off your hand. But everybody know that in advance. So if you steal, na your choice. Every crime get in proper punishment. But if you wait until man commit crime, then you come change the punishment, dat one na foul. Na proper foul. I no know any other country wey dat kin' ting dey happen.

DETIBA. I agree. It's like football. Or any other game. No one changes rules in the middle of a game. Just imagine, half-way through a football game, the referee says the rules have changed. One side has scored a goal but after half-time, he says the net was one inch too wide. Or he says a corner kick which took place ten minutes ago should now be a penalty kick. Can you imagine that? In a mere game it is bad enough, how much more in a matter of life and death.

EMUKE. Only Army mind fit think dat kin' ting.

DETIBA. It's their profession. They don't know the difference between life and death.

EMUKE. Soja man say 'come', soja man say 'go' – everything confuse! You no fit say – A-ah, but na soja man say make I come. The soja man wey tell you 'go' done finish you because you obey soja man 'come'. And if you try Go-come-come-go,; both of them go shoot you together. Den leave your body for checkpoint to show example.

DETIBA. It's the training they get.

EMUKE. Chineke! [*God*.] Small crime wey carry only seven years before. Abi? No to seven years maximum before before? .

DETIBA. Until three days ago. Anyway, it's all a game of

nerves. And the verdict is still subject to appeal. Then the
Eternal Ruling Council takes a final decision.

MIGUEL (*quietly, still at the window*). Not another fool
surely.

DETIBA *and* EMUKE *exchange glances.*

There's a canoe trying to break through the hyacinths. I
can see its lantern.

DETIBA *and* EMUKE *dash to the window and press
together for a good view.*

DETIBA. Come on, champion, come on!

EMUKE. Na sign, I swear, na sign from heaven.

DETIBA. He's more than halfway through already.

Excited shouts from the other PRISONERS *urging on the
lone paddler.*

MIGUEL (*walks away slowly. Sits on the bed*). What he
needs is an assistant wielding a giant pair of water shears,
maybe five yards long.

DETIBA. He seems to be doing quite well without it. Come
on, dig in man, dig in!

EMUKE. 'E go do am. If not today, then tomorrow. The
others go join am try if 'e no manage reach us tonight.

*Loud cheers from the entire length of the wall. Then the
cheers slow down. Change of tone from optimism to defeat.*

DETIBA. He's giving up. He's turning back.

MIGUEL. What did you expect? It was hopeless from the
start.

DETIBA. He's rowed through half of it. You'll see, he'll be
back tomorrow. With others. They'll finish the job
together.

EMUKE (*clasping his hands fervently and looking up in*

supplication). Chineke God! Put power for dem shoulder tomorrow. Put plenty power for all dem legs, arms, necks, backside, blockoss self . . .

MIGUEL. No, it won't happen. We are all trapped where it will never happen. And if it does, we won't be here to see it.

The light fades out in their cell as a MILITARY VOICE *comes over speakers. Light on in general cell.*

MILITARY VOICE. What are the watchwords of our national goal? Discipline, Self Reliance. Self Sufficiency. Vigilance. A nation which bargains away its integrity through indiscipline loses respect in the eyes of the world. A nation which is slack encourages saboteurs against its very existence. Drugs are the bane of society. Expose the dealers among you. It is the duty . . .

The COMMANDANT *is seen haranguing his* INMATES *in sync. with the words emerging from the loudspeaker.*

COMMANDANT (*his booming voice drowns the speakers*). . . . of every citizen to display his curriculum vitae to justify his right to exist among us because Abandon Shame All Who Enter Here. It's paradise before the apple of knowledge. We run an open government and have nothing to hide, no skeletons in the cupboard, no dirty linen in the wash, no fly in the ointment, no mote in thine own eye, no sand-sand in the gari . . .

ADC. Commandant sir, the student is ready with his curriculum vitae.

COMMANDANT. So am I. And tell him he has to pay extra for that prologue I have just improvised. Or opening glee – that's the term we preferred to use in those days.

With chorus-line dancing of course. Hubert Ogunde –
God rest his soul – used to drill us to perfection.

Cuts a quick Ogunde line-up jig with a rendition of 'awa
l'ogboju ole, ti nbe l'eti osa'.*

NUMBER 2. If we don't start now we won't finish before
general inspection. Commandant! Commandant!

COMMANDANT. I've stopped, I've stopped. It's you, Mr
Chief-of-Staff, holding up progress.

*He surrenders centre-stage to another inmate who is
wearing a loose Dansiki over a wrapper. His character is
SEBE IRAWE. Another is seen touching up 'her' eyelashes
and stuffing rags into her 'brassiere'. Others similarly
prepare.*

COMMANDANT (*pointing at the* STUDENT, *he breaks
into a chuckle*). Got himself arrested and gaoled for his
own protection. I tell you, these students are something
else.

His NUMBER 2 *throws him a look of rebuke.*

All right, all right (*Puts a finger across his lips*.) Fe-e-e-
em!

The STUDENT*'s curriculum vitae begins:*

SEBE IRAWE *is at his usual seat behind an open window,
keeping an eye on the world, occasionally traversing his
teeth with a chewing stick. A placard with the words 'Office
Closed' hangs below the window sill. A passing* WOMAN
genuflects, moves briskly on her way. A MAN *half pros-
trates and* SEBE *gives a condescending nod and wave of*

---

*Hubert Ogunde was a famous theatre artiste. In his early days, one
of his hallmarks was a 'can-can' style choreography.

the hand. Yet another approaches, sees SEBE *and spins around, beating a hasty retreat. A* WOMAN *with a tray of goods curtsies, then, as soon as she is out of sight, turns and spits in the direction of the house muttering under her breath. The* INMATES *supply Muslim and Christian chants, punctuated by some household and other noises to indicate a low-income quarter just waking up. Enter, from a new direction, a neatly dressed* WOMAN. *She consults a piece of paper as if to check directions, appears decided and walks to the window.*

WOMAN. My auntie sends you greetings.

SEBE *studies her slowly, spits.*

SEBE. Don't you people sleep in your house?

WOMAN. When the roof itself is robbed of sleep, how can the house dwellers find rest? When last do you think my eyes have known sleep!

SEBE. All right, all right. Don't give me a sermon so early in the morning. I get enough from all these Lemomu and born-again Kiriyo in this neighbourhood. It is getting so a hard-working man cannot get a good night's sleep in his own house.

WOMAN (*more desperately*). My auntie sends you greetings.

SEBE. I heard you the first time. I'm not deaf.

WOMAN. Then you know why I am here. Answer me in God's name. This is the fifth place I have been in the past week. I said, my auntie . . .

SEBE (*raises his hand to stop her*). My grandfather returns her greetings. (*Ostentatious glance at his non-existent watch.*) It's well before my opening hours, you know. You're making me work overtime before my day has even begun.

WOMAN. She says she lost something in the market place.

SEBE. Right. That will do. I suppose you will like to look at the family album (*gets up*.) How long did this loss take place?

WOMAN. Two weeks. Exactly two weeks ago.

SEBE (*nods*). All right. Wait here. I'll go get the album.

The WOMAN *clutches her hands together, obviously under intense emotional stress. Raises her face to the heavens and appears to say a silent prayer. The* STUDENT *approaches. His eyes are bloodshot and his hands twitch.*

STUDENT. Isn't he up yet?

The WOMAN *is startled. She recovers herself and studies the quivering object before her.*

WOMAN. Who?

The STUDENT *cranes his neck through the window, as if searching the interior of the house. The* WOMAN *retreats a step or two.*

STUDENT. Baba, Baba o. Sebe Baba.

SEBE (*from inside*). If that voice belongs to the scum I think it does, let its owner not let me set eyes on him when I return.

STUDENT. It's all right Baba, it's all right. I have money. I have it right here. (*Starts pulling notes out of his pockets.*)

SEBE (*re-enters with album. Looks the young man up and down*). You have money, you said?

STUDENT. Right here. (*Piles the notes on the window-sill.*)

SEBE. I see. And who did you kill to find so much money?

STUDENT (*attempting some measure of dignity*). I am not
a murderer. And anyway, since when have you concerned
yourself with how people get their money?

SEBE. I'll tell you since when.

*A seemingly disembodied arm makes a swift grab for the
young man's head, and yanks it round, drops the album.
SEBE's other forearm pins the STUDENT's neck against
the window sill. SEBE grabs the money and begins to stuff
the open mouth with the notes.*

It is since the spoilt, good-for-nothing children of rich
socialites like you began to get mixed up in other people's
business. You are born with a silver spoon in your mouth,
but that is not enough for you. You have to dip it in our
own soup-pot, and without first learning our table man-
ners. And then you acquire dirty habits. And that leads to
dirty money . . .

STUDENT (*choking*). Sebe Baba . . . please, please . . .

SEBE. Just take a good look of this water side! The
government says it cannot get rid of the weeds. They've
tried everything but the stuff keeps growing, growing and
spreading all over the place. Do you want to know why?

STUDENT. Please Chief, please . . . I'm choking.

SEBE. He's choking. I tell you the lagoon is choking. And
you haven't even asked why. Ask me why, monkey, ask
Sebe to tell you why. I said, ask!

STUDENT. Why, Chief, Why?

SEBE. That's better. I'll tell you why. It is thanks to
excrement like you. Because that is where you end up.
With all the other excrement which they flush into the
lagoon. As long as the water weed has plenty of your type
to feed on, all those so-and-so marine specialists or
whatever they call them, they are wasting their time.
There is far too much shit like you, waiting to pass

through the sewage pipes and nourish the hyacinths. Have
you got that?

STUDENT. Yes, Chief, yes.

SEBE (*barks*). Chief what? Maybe that's your trouble.
Because there are Chiefs and Chiefs but do you remind
yourself which kind of Chief you are dealing with? So tell
me, what am I called? What is the name that comes after
my own Paramount Chiefiness?

STUDENT. I don't get you Chief – please. My throat. I
can't breathe . . .

SEBE *relaxes grip but keeps a firm hold on the*
STUDENT's *head, shoving it backwards and forwards
and sideways, pressing down on his skull as the mood takes
him.*

SEBE. Don't understand what? You know my name don't
you? You know what they call me?

STUDENT. Yes Chief, who doesn't?

SEBE. Well, go on. Tell me. What do they call me? How am
I known from Badagry to Ilorin and even down Eastern
side Cameroon border? Those who seek me out, those
people who are sent to me for help, who do they ask for?
What name do they whisper?

STUDENT (*hesitant*). Sebe. Chief Sebe.

SEBE (*affably*). No-o-o. Call out the full ting. Give a man
his proper name. Sebe wetin.

STUDENT. Se-be Irawe.

SEBE. Louder, louder, use your throat. You think it is a
name to be ashamed of? Is that why you are whispering it
like a dirty secret? What comes after Irawe? Call it out for
the world to hear!

STUDENT. That is . . . that is all I know Chief.

SEBE (*stares at him for a moment, as if he is about to
explode, then calms down*). We-e-ell. I suppose I mustn't

be too harsh on his ignorance. He can't know everything can he? University is all very well, but they don't teach them about their own heroes over there. (*Chuckles*.) My boy, let me explain something to you – no, first of all, let me make sure you even know the meaning of that name. Go on, tell us. Let's hear if they haven't completely washed your brain clean of your own mother tongue. What is Sebe?

STUDENT. Sebe is a kind of snake, Chief . . .

SEBE. A kind of name, a kind of snake – what is that? What kind of snake? Have you ever seen one?

STUDENT. I only know it's dangerous kind, Chief. Deadly.

SEBE. The pupil knows something. Deadly, that's right. Deadly. And then – Irawe?

STUDENT. Leaves, Chief. The leaves on the ground.

SEBE. A-ha! That's where you are wrong. Hn-hn. Don't argue with me. Just listen. Yes, irawe is the leaves on the ground. The innocent leaves which make sebe even more deadly because it hides underneath them. It lies in wait. Until you step on it. Then – you don't even hear the rustle. You don't even know that something has pinched you. But one minute later (*Chuckles*.) you no longer know where you are, who you are. So much for that one. But suppose it is not that kind of irawe? Suppose the leaves we are talking about, what soja-man calls camouflage, suppose it is not leaves on the ground at all, but that other kind which covers up the lagoon? Suppose that is the kind of irawe under which Sebe is hiding?

STUDENT. I still don't get you Chief.

SEBE (*mimicking*). I don't get you Chief . . . Of course you don't get me. You can't get me because you don't know my full title. Sebe Irawe Oju odo, yes. I know you're hearing it for the first time. My kind of Sebe doesn't wait for you on land. It waits in the water. Under leaf. Over leaf. Under lake. Over lake. Under sea. Over sea . . . Over sea . . . overseas. Are you getting me or am I too deep for you? Can you swim? Are you drowning?

With a sudden motion SEBE *renews his grip on the* STUDENT's *throat.*

SEBE. Now, my package. What did you do with my package?

The STUDENT's *gurgle is inaudible.* SEBE *slackens his grip a little.*

Speak. I'm listening. The package you say you delivered overseas. I say what did you do with it?

STUDENT. I delivered . . . I swear . . . I delivered . . .

Stuffing the last note in the STUDENT's *mouth,* SEBE *gives him a powerful shove. The* STUDENT *sprawls on the ground, choking.*

SEBE. They think they are so clever. Because they have been to University, they think they know everything. Listen to me, you leftover of Oro's breakfast – because that is all you are. And less, much much less if that package is not handed back to me within the next seven days. The package, or the money. Now listen! The man to whom you say you delivered the goods in Milan, he was in prison at the time. We have made contact with him. He was arrested the day before your plane touched Rome. We know everything. He managed to arrange for a friend to meet you. That one gave the correct password and you went with him. But you split the package between the two of you. You conspired to say that your contact was caught *after* you had delivered the goods to him. We know everything, scum.

STUDENT. He's lying. Wherever he is, he's lying!

SEBE. Your partner in crime has confessed his own part.
You see, your type is very stupid. That's the difference
between you and your accomplice. He was tempted, he
fell. Even Adam our forefather was not perfect. But your
contact knew it couldn't last forever. He borrowed the
stuff, that's what he did. Borrowed it. Made himself some
bread. He knew he had to pay it back sooner or later. So
when our people over there caught up with him, he
tendered. Guilty with reason, he pleaded. But they told
him, no, guilty with interest. They calculated the interest.
He paid back the capital. And he paid the interest. But
you, what did you do with your capital?

The WOMAN *has been watching, fascinated partly by the
scene but also by the small album which* SEBE *has left on
the window sill.*

STUDENT. Give me time. But please, right now, give me
. . . just to keep going. I will find the money and settle
everything.

WOMAN. Baba, please, my own matter . . .

SEBE. Oh madam, sorry. It's this sort of people who give
decent business a bad name. And to come here to pollute
my presence first thing in the morning. Take. (*Hands her
the album.*) Just go through the photos and see if you find
your auntie's missing property in there. As for you, seven
days, that's all. Any fool who wants to do business knows
that the first law is that you don't eat your capital. You did
worse. You sniffed it. Injected it into your bloodstream.
That's the way it is with amateurs. Especially when they
think they know book.

STUDENT. It's not like that Baba . . .

SEBE. You are dirtying my office you know. Everybody
knows I keep regular hours. Seven-thirty sharp and I am

open to the public. That's in ten minutes. I've only attended this madam because I felt sorry for her. So I don't want to see your face here when I open up office. Don't give my business a bad reputation.

There is a gasp from the WOMAN, *who has been rapidly turning the pages of the album. At the same time she sits down in a heap and takes her head in her hands, swaying.*

SEBE. Ah Madam, you have found the missing goods?

The WOMAN *nods, her head still held in her hands.*

God is great. Which one is it? Show us, show us.

She gets up slowly. Trembling, she holds out the album at the open page, raises it towards SEBE.

You! I said take your carcass out of here. Are you deaf? Or shall I feed you to the water weeds right now?

The STUDENT *stumbles off. He does not go far however.*

WOMAN. The young woman on the right. My youngest sister.

SEBE (*looks at the picture, then at the* WOMAN). It has a cross against it.

WOMAN. What . . . does that mean?

SEBE. I am sorry. You seem a nice person. I feel very sorry for you . . .

WOMAN (*screaming*). What does it mean?

SEBE. Now, now, calm yourself. Remember, this is an office. We don't allow people to shout and scream as if they're in the market.

WOMAN (*with difficulty*). Please . . . what . . . does . . . it . . . mean?

SEBE. And it isn't as if it's the end of the world. I can close this album and that means I have closed your file. Full stop. You came here for information. Whatever you do, remember you always need more information. Even if the goods have been damaged beyond repair, you still need to know where it is kept, don't you? Better bear that in mind.

WOMAN (*nods miserably*). Tell me, I beg you.

SEBE. That's better. We are all human after all. Those who do these things, they have no heart. If they have any, it must be like stone. But they need us, just as you need us. Somebody has to act as go-between, otherwise there won't be a chance for any kind of remedy. This way, they come to us, we put the word out to the next-of-kin and so on. That's all we are – go-betweens. Of course if the police were doing their job properly, we wouldn't be needed. No one would have any use for us. But I don't have to tell you, even the Police send people to us. People go to report to the Police but the Police don't even bother to open a file. They know your best bet is to come to us. We keep proper files.

WOMAN. The cross. Please, the cross. Tell me what it means.

SEBE. Oh, the cross. You know what a cross means – rest in peace. (*Gestures across the throat.*) You people were slow. You should have moved faster. I mean, she was a successful businesswoman.

WOMAN. It was a lot of money they were asking. We tried to borrow. We sold possessions . . .

SEBE. I know, I know. As I said, I feel very sorry for you. But those people, I tell you, sometimes I think they don't even know their own mothers. Well?

WOMAN. Where will I find . . . ?

SEBE. Ah yes of course, you will need to give her a decent burial won't you? Now let's see. Well, shall we say – ten?

WOMAN. Ten thousand?

SEBE. That's the charge. It's a risky business all round,

you'll appreciate. Even the Police get nasty with us from time to time. You know, somebody high up turns up the heat, and that burns down to our level sooner or later. They have to make a scapegoat here and there. When the oga is appeased, things cool down again and we continue business as usual. (*Looks at his watch.*) Ah, excuse me.

Turns the placard round so it now reads: 'Open For Business'.

WOMAN (*she has taken out five bundles*). That is ten thousand.

SEBE (*scribbles on a scrap of paper*). I won't bother to count it. As I said, I like you as a person. I can tell an honest face when I see one. (*Hands her the paper.*) Go to this address.

WOMAN (*struggling to control herself*). Will I find . . . is that where she's kept?

SEBE. Oh no. Even I don't know that. I don't want to know. I have to protect myself. What you don't know, you can't tell. When you get to that address, someone will take you to her last resting-place.

WOMAN. Who do I ask for? What do I say?

SEBE. No one. No password this time, nothing to say. When you knock on the door, just hand over the piece of paper to whoever opens the door. There will be a driver to take you to the place – that's where all the money goes you know. So many facilities to provide. Well, goodbye. My condolences. Take it as the will of God. Don't brood too much.

Dragging her feet, the WOMAN *leaves. As soon as the role player is offstage, he begins to unstuff himself. The others slap him on the back to say 'well done'.* SEBE *sighs, begins to count the money. The* COMMANDANT *appears with exaggerated furtiveness, head down as if to avoid* *recognition. His voluminous agbada* gives the same suggestion. As soon as* SEBE *catches sight of him, he shuts the window. Opens it again in order to change the placard to 'Office Closed', but leaves the window open.*

'Song of the Social Prophylactic', sung by SEBE. *All* INMATES *join in the chorus 'Man must wack'.*

Song of the Social Prophylactic
   Before you start to look at me
   So censorious
   Just remember it's all basic –
      Man must wack

   The issue is quite plain to see
   Nothing mysterious
   The Law of flesh is not romantic –
      Man must wack

   Some methods may appear to be
   A touch nefarious
   But civilian stooge or soldier's sidekick –
      Man must wack

   Rulers are deemed by you and me
   Meritorious
   They do their job for a safe republic –
      Man must wack

   Civil law or stern decree
   So imperious
   The private sector remains elastic –
      Man must wack

   The question to be or not to be
   Is precarious

*Agbada: item of clothing worn by the Yoruba

Leave all morals to the cleric –
  Man must wack

Why must we make the obvious plea
Acrimonious
It takes all kinds, both cool and manic –
  Man must wack

Between us we will all agree
On a serious –
Minded approach to the psychopathic –
  Man must wack

My task is thus to oversee
All the worriers
Finding peace in place of heartache –
  Man must wack

And so for a very modest fee
Parsimonious
I act as a social prophylactic –
  Man must wack

Sometimes the case is beyond all plea
So lugubrious
But then isn't life sometimes erratic?
  Man must wack

Let's raise a toast to our control-free
And so glorious
Never-say-die-till-you're-dead Republic –
  Man must wack!

The stranger hurries past the window which SEBE *again closes.*

During the song, the scene is swiftly altered to indicate the interior of SEBE's *home – a few armchairs, one with an outsize cushion in velvet cover – one of those gaudy covers with a Far-Eastern motif. SEBE himself begins to fuss with the cushions halfway through, as if dissatisfied with his furnishing. Finally he leaves everything as it was, with a smug, self-satisfied smile. Rushes forward at the end of the song to usher in his visitor.*

The STUDENT has been watching his motions. He moves nearer and takes up position near the door after the visitor has entered.

SEBE. Come in Commander. My dear Wing Commander, do come in. I didn't know you were back.

WING COMMANDER (*glances round sharply*). I've told you not to use my rank in public.

SEBE (*calmly*). We're alone. Besides, there are hundreds of Commanders – Air Force, Navy, Civil Defence – name it. Even the Salvation Army. They are outnumbered only by Generals. In any case, no one recognises you people out of uniform. You become mortals, just like the rest of us.

WING COMMANDER. Just the same, I'd feel better if you learnt to avoid it.

SEBE. Of course, of course. Make yourself at home. When did you return?

WING COMMANDER. I'm coming straight from the airport.

SEBE. Good God, you must be tired. You'd better have something. I know it's never too early for . . .

WING COMMANDER. I didn't come here for a drink, Chief. I am not happy with the situation.

SEBE. Happy? Who is happy, my friend? Who can be happy these days when there is so much unhappiness in the world. And the economic – ah – situation! If you only knew what suffering surrounds one here. There was a woman this morning for instance . . .

WING COMMANDER. I have not come to talk about a woman either. I want the latest report. What is going on?

SEBE. Nothing Chief, that's the trouble. Nothing. *There – is – no – action*. None whatever.

WING COMMANDER. That was the same report you sent me in Karachi and I'll tell you straight away, I can't accept it.

SEBE (*quiet menace*). You don't believe me, Commander?

WING COMMANDER (*hastily*). Not you. Don't take everything so personally. I'm talking about your boys. Your scouts. Either they are incompetent or they are dishonest. Such a heavy consignment cannot simply have vanished into thin air.

SEBE. Of course it cannot my dear friend. It is somewhere on firm land. Hidden away. Waiting. It's all a question of how long the rogues can wait.

WING COMMANDER. They don't have to wait! There is no stamp on that commodity. You break it up, re-package it and sell it off through the usual channels. No one simply sits on stuff like that. People get rid of it as fast as they can.

SEBE. No chief, you've got it wrong. Fifty kilograms! Neatly packaged in one fertilizer bag. Just think, if one were able to sell such a consignment intact! A one-shot deal. No middlemen. No messy distribution. No waste. I think we are dealing with a master planner, someone with heavy international contacts. Definitely a master planner.

WING COMMANDER. Someone like you?

SEBE (*pause. Then a big sigh*). Commander, it is the military who produce master planners. You plan all the coups. What time do we others have for planning, we miserable dregs of society who merely try to earn a dishonest living?

WING COMMANDER (*nervous smile*). Oh come on, I've told you, you're too touchy. That was meant to be a compliment. As a schemer, you can teach even us officers a trick or two. I know you Sebe, don't forget I know you.

SEBE (*rises abruptly*). Let me give you a drink my friend. I don't believe in these overnight flights, even for a seasoned pilot like you. In fact, I don't believe in flights at all, over night or over day. That last flight I took to Jeddah on pilgrimage . . .

WING COMMANDER. You did? I didn't know you were an Alhaji. So there are things even I don't know about you.

SEBE. Well Chief, I don't use the title . . . Whisky and Campari, right?

WING COMMANDER. All right. You know the proportions.

SEBE (*setting about the drinks*). There has to be some honesty in the world, whatever people say. How can I call myself Alhaji? It wouldn't be right. I went to Saudi, I went to Jeddah on pilgrimage, but it was strictly a business pilgrimage. I am not a Moslem. Or rather, I am a Moslem. But I am also a Christian, Bhuddist, traditionalist worshipper . . . everything you like, and none of them at the same time. How then can I honestly call myself an Alhaji?

WING COMMANDER. You are impossible.

SEBE. No my friend, you are wrong. I am possible. I am very possible. Perhaps the most possible businessman in this our corner of the world. Here you are. Drink it down and the world will begin to look better.

WING COMMANDER (*morosely. Sets down the glass without drinking*). I wish it were that easy. There is unprecedented investment on the loose and we don't seem to be able to rope it in.

SEBE. Give it time. This thing is just like pregnancy. After a while there is no wrapper in the world which can hide it.

WING COMMANDER. I'm losing face. Every day that

passes, I lose face. I gave assurances. I assured them in Pakistan that we were in total control over here. Nothing could go wrong. What do you imagine? That fifty kilo-grams at one go would be shipped out on the personal guarantee of one man?

SEBE. There is always a risk involved.

WING COMMANDER. Not between governments.

SEBE. Between governments? What are you saying, Commander?

WING COMMANDER. What? Oh, it's not what you imagine. No, what I mean is . . . the people involved over there, my counterparts, they are in government. To deal with them on an equal level, I had to make them believe that it was a government to government affair. That there was cooperation here at the very highest level.

SEBE. Well there is. You are still on the Eternal Ruling Council.

WING COMMANDER. Yes, that was why they approached me in the first place. Even though I went there on one of those courses, almost a student so to speak, the fact that I was on the Ruling Council — well, I had the full VIP treatment. But the real stroke of luck was getting on with the President himself. He took to me, told me to make his palace my second home. I would drop in for a meal or a drink, without notice.

SEBE. This is wonderful! You mean you actually met that tough man Zia?

WING COMMANDER (*amused, and also a little puzz-led*). What do you know about the rulers of countries like Pakistan? (*He starts to sip his drink.*)

SEBE. Only what we read in the papers, Commander, only what we hear on radio or watch on television. I tell you, that Zia man impressed me! The way he ignored every-body's protests and actually hanged a Prime Minister of his own country. This Prime Minister who studied in Oxford – or was it Cambridge? I mean to say, Commander, this Bhutto was even his country's representative to the United Nations. And Mr Zia hanged him – just like that. Hanged him like a common murderer! (*Chuckles to himself.*) I tell you Commander, you soldiers are wonderful people!

WING COMMANDER. What is so wonderful about that? He broke the laws, and he was given a fair trial . . .

SEBE. Fair trial: Haba, my good friend! According to my lawyer friends . . .

WING COMMANDER. According to the laws of the land, he was found guilty of murder. He arranged the murder of one of his political opponents. The highest court in the land found him guilty, what more do you want?

SEBE. The laws of the land, Commander? My friend, we know how you people make and unmake laws to suit yourselves. It's our business to know, or we can't be in business. Not that we're complaining but, Commander, look at it from a businessman's point of view. All right? Now let's say I make the same deal in Kótópó as in Kòtòpò.* In Kótópó, the punishment is two years suspended sentence, while in Kòtòpò – (*Gestures across his throat.*) That's Army government for you, all inside one country like this one. And it doesn't end there. When one started that very business deal, Alhaji Kótópó was in charge, but then, you wake up the next morning and General Kòtòpò has taken over in Pòtòko and the rules are changed overnight. Everything becomes Kótópó-Kòtòpò-

*Kótópó/Kòtòpò etc. This is a Yoruba play on words where different accents provide infinite meanings and sometimes no meaning at all. The 'meaning' then is that whatever situation is being described has neither head nor tail.

Kótópó and you find yourself floundering in pòtòpótó. Well, that's our business life for you but, I mean, it's not fair. It lacks stability and without stability you can't do business.

WING COMMANDER. Sebe Irawe, I leave business philosophy to you. All I can tell you is that this Bhutto, your so-called civilian democrat, was found guilty of abusing his power to commit a capital felony, and he paid the price.

SEBE. But only according to the rules of your man, General Kótópó Zia. One moment, it was one kind of law, then the next day, his people came in . . .

WING COMMANDER. You are very confused, Sebe. Zia merely applied Islamic Law, and that is constant. Bhutto was free to do the same when he was in charge. Anyway, why go all the way to Pakistan when . . .

SEBE. Commander, I am not the person who went to Pakistan. You did, not me.

WING COMMANDER. You know what I am talking about! Zia, Zia, Zia! What did Zia do which you bloody civilians haven't done here? I mean, you are beginning to sound like all these University types . . .

SEBE. Is that my fault? They do business with me all the time, they and their tiroro* children. If the leaf sticks too long to the soap, it will soon start to froth on its own.

WING COMMANDER. Well, the next time one of them comes here, ask him what happened to Diallo Telli. Yes, let your acada† friends tell you what happened to the first-ever Secretary-General of the OAU, the Organisation of African Unity.

---

*Tiroro means spoilt, affected and alienated children, usually products of foreign upbringing.
†Acada = *academic*.

SEBE. What happened to him?

WING COMMANDER. Tortured to death by Sekou Touré's goons. And Sekou Touré was not Army. Or Navy. Or Air Force. He was a civilian.

SEBE. All right all right, I don't know why we dey argue self.

WING COMMANDER (*flaring up*). We are arguing because I am tired of having everything blamed on us military people. Between Sekou Touré and General Zia or Pinochet or Arap Moi and Houphouet Boigny and other one-party African and Asian dictators, tell me, just what is the difference?

SEBE *shrugs*.

Well, go on, Chief. You know so much of world affairs, so, tell us the difference?

SEBE. When my varsity people come, I will ask them. I can't answer you right now.

WING COMMANDER. Yes, you do that. Pose that question to your garrulous eggheads!

SEBE (*anxious to mend fences*). Who thought up the fertilizer bags, Commander – as if I need to ask?

WING COMMANDER (*smiles*). Nothing to it. I said to Zia – why not send us a fraternal gift of a thousand bags of fertilizer – you know, as a gesture of friendship. A contribution to our Operation Feed-The-Nation. Of course he agreed. The rest was easy – special Presidential consignment. Privileged cargo, no question, no inspection. The generals took care of their end. Easy. I was supposed to do the same with ours.

SEBE. God punish those pirates!

WING COMMANDER. I'm afraid we can't wait on God, Chief. You find them, and I'll guarantee their punishment right here! And fast!

SEBE. God willing, we'll find them. Such beautiful work, so neat my Commander, God won't allow it to go to waste. Or let other people reap where they haven't sown.

WING COMMANDER. The consignment must be found, Chief. Those pirates have wives. They have girlfriends. They visit bars, brothels. They relax in marijuana dens. They talk. They must talk. This kind of consignment is without precedent in these parts, indeed, anywhere except Colombia. Nobody can sit on it without someone knowing and talking.

SEBE. Chief, you'd be surprised. We'll find it. We'll track it down but, you'd be surprised. An elephant could go to ground in Lagos. It could vanish between Idumota and Iganmu, in full view of everyone, and no one would have seen it happen. Someone could be sitting on it in Alaba market, or using it for a pillow . . . (*His eyes dart to the outsize cushion, very briefly.*)

WING COMMANDER. This is different. Nobody can sit on it without burning a hole in his bottom – not in this country!

SEBE. Commander, I must hand it to you. When it comes the Big League, we civilians are simply outclassed. Fifty kilograms at one stroke. Oh, I forgot to thank you for helping out with that affair in Milan. Your minder at the Embassy got through to the courier in prison. We got the full picture. Our own man is back in the country. He has seven days, and then they will pick up his bloated corpse in the lagoon.

The STUDENT *reacts. The slight noise is overheard by the two men.*

WING COMMANDER. I thought you said we were alone.

SEBE. Of course we are.

WING COMMANDER. But the noise. I heard something.

SEBE. Probably some neighbourhood chicken, scratching for its livelihood. Same as me my friend, same as me.

The WING COMMANDER *shakes his head, puts a finger to his lips and begins to tiptoe to the door. He yanks it open, confronting the* STUDENT *who jumps up but seems too petrified to run.*

SEBE. Well, well, well, if it isn't still what the sea washed up on my frontage. You pail of garbage, didn't I warn you to stop polluting my neighbourhood? Vanish!

The STUDENT *runs off.*

WING COMMANDER. Who is he? What was he doing here?

SEBE. That's him. That's the scum who tried to double-cross Sebe Irawe.

WING COMMANDER. You mean your courier? The Milan business?

SEBE. The same. He must have been scared to death when he heard me say . . .

Stops dead and stares at his partner. The WING COMMANDER *nods slowly.*

The bastard! He was eavesdropping!!

WING COMMANDER. No doubt about it.

SEBE (*wide-eyed with disbelief*). I thought at first he was simply desperate for a fix – that's why he wouldn't go away. (*Nearly screaming.*) Eavesdropping on me? In my very house? All right, I'll fix him. His seven day reprieve is off! (*His eyes dart to the cushion.*) Spying on me! He had probably been at it before you came in!

WING COMMANDER. Hey, you look almost scared to death, Chief. What have you been up to?

SEBE. Me scared? What for? It's the principle of the thing.

It's indecent. Is a man no longer entitled to some privacy in his own home? I mean, my friend, what is the country coming to?

WING COMMANDER. Chief, I am more concerned with what he may have overheard since we started talking.

SEBE. So am I, my friend, so am I. But put your mind at rest. Whatever food the frog has eaten, it is still the snake which digests it in the end. Leave it to me.

WING COMMANDER. But will you find him soon enough, before he does any damage?

SEBE. Will I find him soon enough? (*Laughs*.) Does the snail leave a trail of slime wherever it drags itself? The trail left by a drug addict looking for a fix is wider than the Lagos-Ibadan expressway. My friend, forget that object you saw just now. He is dead. Before you reach your office this morning, he has become part of the ooze of the nearest compost heap. Sebe Irawe does not waste time. Let's talk of better things.

WING COMMANDER. Well, don't let me regret that I cracked that case for you. If that brat proves to be the knife with which we cut our own throats, it would be a funny way of repaying me.

SEBE (*affably*). Commander, we are all grateful. The way your 'special services' in the Embassies responded – but of course we expected nothing less. You think we can forget the old London exploit?

WING COMMANDER. What about London?

SEBE. That Scotland Yard affair. Just when it looked as if some top people were in the soup . . . (*He gives a prolonged chuckle*.) We were impressed. Two diplomatic bags full of marijuana, intercepted by Scotland Yard. Scotland Yard swings into action, delivers the bags to our High Commission where they are put in the basement strong room. They thought they were setting a clever trap.

Fi-o-o-om! The bags disappear. No trace! An official of
the Embassy dies a mysterious death. In his own apart-
ment. Very mysterious. I tell you Commander, we were
most impressed. Very impressed. We held a meeting and
we decided, these are people with whom we can do
business. These are serious people. They know when a
bargain is a bargain.

WING COMMANDER. Then perhaps you understand the
gravity of my position.

SEBE. Say no more my Commander, say no more. Even in
our modest world, we know. When you promise to
deliver, you deliver. And you cover your tracks. Even if it
means burning down the Ministry of External Affairs back
home.

The WING COMMANDER *reacts, then shrugs and
remains silent.*

Commander, I said, wasn't it a strange coincidence? The
timing made one wonder. The papers, even the government confirmed that the crucial report was on its way,
from Scotland Yard. It was coming in the diplomatic
bag . . .

WING COMMANDER. So, a fire breaks out? What's so
remarkable about that?

SEBE. Quite right Chief, nothing at all remarkable. Naturally, that was the end of the whole matter. Apart from
another Nigerian corpse which was fished out of that River
Thames of London.

WING COMMANDER. Who says there was any connection?

SEBE. Not me my friend, not me. The matter died. Even
Scotland Yard got the message and retired. I mean, after

all, they had done their own part. Our usually noisy
journalists got bored – or scared. The comments petered
out. I tell you Commander, when you people are involved
in our business, we know we are safe.

WING COMMANDER (*laughing*). No, no, no. Let's give
credit where credit is due. Maybe somebody at the
London embassy placed an incendiary device in the
diplomatic bag, why blame us?

SEBE. Incendiary device – is that what it was?

WING COMMANDER. I am theorising, like everybody
else. If somebody could replace the entire contents of a
diplomatic bag with Indian hemp, why couldn't that same
someone plant an incendiary device in another bag? You
know how it works.

SEBE. No, I don't . . .

WING COMMANDER (*settling instinctively into professional tone*). There are different kinds. For instance,
one method, as soon as the bag is opened to to fresh air . . .
oh go away! What can you understand about those
technical matters!

SEBE. You're right my friend, you are quite right. A
diplomatic bag which contrabands, deserves to conflag-
rate . . .

SEBE *and the* WING COMMANDER *sing the Song of
the Diplomatic Bag.*

For a diplomatic bag
Is a most elastic bag
It can stretch to hold an elephant
Or a full electric plant
Plenipotentiary pack
It will cover every track
And for any busybody wag
It'll serve as a body bag.

The famous Scotland Yard
Its record yet unmarred
Did smell a rat in a diplomat's pouch
Which raised a sleuthy grouch
A crack team did they field
Round the strongroom barred and sealed
But the pouch from the land of the vanishing trick
Had sailed through stone and brick.

The Yardmen undeterred
Their detective passion stirred
They followed the trail of a prime suspect
And soon his flat was checked
They found him safe in bed
Diplomatically dead
Of the missing bags nor clue nor trace
The Yard had lost the race.

This went against the grain
The guilty hand was plain
The dossier went to their distant client
The Yard would not relent
But the show was merely passed
To a different stage and cast
And a different audience now would cheer
The transatlantic fare.

So away four thousand miles
Their investigative files
In the Ministry of Foreign Affairs
Went up in glorious flares
In vain the Fire Brigade
Did race to render aid
The steel-lined confidential store
Was razed to the concrete floor.

For a diplomatic bag
Is a copious magic bag
It's free from drug-free guarantee
To contraband it's free
Its mouth is open wide
To swallow nation pride
For though it stink in a foreign state
The bag is a sovereign state.

Cell 'C'. MIGUEL *speaks as the cell is spotlit.* DETIBA *and* EMUKE *are playing draughts.*

MIGUEL (*violently*). It makes you sick! Any way you look at it, it really is sickening. They're doing it to gain favour with Reagan, that bloody hypocrite! All of them, bloody hypocrites. Do they shoot their own people? No way. They slap them on the wrist with a few years . . .

DETIBA. Which they hardly ever complete.

MIGUEL. Yes, parole takes care of most of it. They do a fraction of the sentence and they get out on parole. But here they shed innocent blood to satisfy the Knight Crusader. Those damned hypocrites know where the stuff is traded like salt, where it changes hands like local currency. The Americans turn a blind eye on the Mujahe-din in Afghanistan because they're fighting communist rule. In North Pakistan you can buy an armoured tank with a packet of the stuff and collect your change with a mortar or two. So why do we have to shoot one another over here? What the hell are we trying to prove?

DETIBA. And what they call prison life over there – television, outdoor games, well stocked libraries . . . I know about some prisons where you can order food from your favourite restaurant.

EMUKE. You done go prison for America?

DETIBA. Not yet.

EMUKE. Na so you say. How come you know so much about American prisons?

DETIBA. I read, Emuke, I read. Pick up an American newspaper any week and you'll read about a prisoner suing the prison for not providing him a woman for the weekend.

EMUKE. Sho!

DETIBA. It's true. Some prisons actually arrange conjugal visits on a regular basis.

EMUKE. Conju wetin?

DETIBA. Conjugal. Visit by wife or fiancée.

EMUKE. Well, I begin sabbe why one friend wey me and in dey do business, every time, 'e go pray say, if one day dey must to catch am, make 'e happen for America.

MIGUEL. Don't bet too heavily on America. Some of their prisons make this one look like Sheraton Hotel.

EMUKE. No way!

MIGUEL. It's true just the same. Especially down South. In some places, they say it's foretaste of hell. (*Stops abruptly, staring straight ahead. Speaks more slowly.*) Hell! Just imagine if there actually were such a place!

EMUKE *and* DETIBA *study* MIGUEL *for some moments, exchange looks.*

EMUKE (*conspiratorially*). 'In mood just change like this. (*Flipping over his hand rapidly.*)

DETIBA. Play.

They make a few moves on the board. In distant background, the muffled sound of foghorns.

EMUKE. Is as if to say the Harmattan never go away yet. All that mist – na because of 'am the ship dey blow foghorn.

DETIBA. This morning when I looked out, I couldn't see down to the lagoon. Even the hyacinths had been swallowed up.

EMUKE. Is good to be on board ship when fog dey. Everything around you, 'e dey just like cotton wool. Sometime you no fit see another man for deck. You are walking like this, and then a body begin commot like ghost. You wake up in the morning and look through porthole, and 'e be like say you dey inside cloud. All the sound for inside ship become soft like dey done wrap every iron with cotton wool. Even the ship bell . . .

DETIBA. So for how many years were you a sailor?

EMUKE. Nearly fifteen years. And nearly all the time with Nkrumah's Black Star Line. I meet Nkrumah one time. He come inspect ship and we all line up salute am for deck. I done run become deckhand since I be small picken. Long before those foolish generals come take over.

DETIBA. Were you in Ghana at the time?

EMUKE. Na China we dey when 'e happen. The Black Star dey go nearly everywhere. But we return home soon after coup. When I see how things begin spoil, I return here come join Elder Dempster Lines. De thing wey dem general do enh . . .

DETIBA. Their throats were too vast. One of them even swallowed a whole ship.

EMUKE. One whole ship? I never hear dat one.

DETIBA. Well, not altogether. Let's just say, he swallowed its cargo. Took care of the entire load – it was cocoa. You remember what cocoa meant to Ghana? What he did was like sucking all the blood from an infant.

EMUKE. I know. We dey carry cocoa go Sweden, London, Turkey, even Russia self.

DETIBA. Ghana didn't have much else. No petrol, no minerals.

EMUKE. They get small gold. I know, because I dey smuggle am commot for some businesswoman one time.

DETIBA. Ancient history. That's when the country still deserved the name Gold Coast.

EMUKE. Dem still dey dig am for some region o. Upper Volta still produce enough for regular business.

DETIBA. But not enough to matter for the country, that's what I'm telling you. For a few people like your businesswoman, yes, but it just didn't affect the nation's economy. Not like cocoa.

EMUKE. Na true.

DETIBA. Cocoa. Every year. What the government watched was the price of cocoa on the world market. And this general, he sold off nearly one-third of the year's harvest and deposited the money in his overseas account.

EMUKE. Chineke God!

DETIBA. Chineke God indeed. Because Chineke God was waiting for him. Very patiently.

EMUKE. Den catch am?

DETIBA. Oh yes. He was one of those they lined up and shot after the second coup. Or third. Or fourth, I forget which. But the people got their pound of flesh in the end.

EMUKE. Make all of dem dey shoot one another self. When no soja lef' the people go get chance rule demselves without dem wahala.

DETIBA. Well, the way they carry on, maybe they are trying to carry out your wish. Coup today, casualties right and left, executions tomorrow. Then another attempt the day after. And then sometimes, you don't even know who is really guilty of something or whether someone is just trying to settle old scores. That Ghana bloodbath for instance, till today many people say that one general was simply shot out of revenge. He wasn't found guilty of anything.

EMUKE. En-hen! Who beg am go mix himself up with gov'men?

DETIBA. Politicians.

EMUKE. Politicians. Na politicians invite am?

DETIBA. They mess up. That's what leads the army into temptation.

EMUKE. Politicians na civilians. Make soja man change to civilians if 'e wan do gov'men'. Dem soja too, dey no de mess up? Dey all wan chop, das all. Anyway, for civilian mess and soja mess, give me civilian mess any time. At least civilian no fit do de kin' dabaru nonsense wey put we for dis kin' mess. (*Pushes the board away.*) I done tire self. (*Walks away from the board and flings himself on the bed.*)

DETIBA (*approaching footsteps*). Now who was accusing somebody just now of being moody? I think we have company.

EMUKE (*sits up quickly*). Na warder?

DETIBA. Who else? (*Looks through the bars.*) It's a new face.

EMUKE (*to* MIGUEL). Make we try this one?

MIGUEL *hasn't heard.*

Mr Domingo!

MIGUEL. What?

DETIBA. There's a new warder. You want us to try him or not? Your letter.

MIGUEL. Oh, sure. Why not? Go ahead.

EMUKE *quickly resumes his place at the draught board. The* WARDER *strolls in, inspects the* INMATES *and watches the two players make a few moves.*

WARDER. Good morning. Hm. I see you people sabbe play draught o.

EMUKE (*without looking up*). I see you get eyes for your head.

WARDER. Haba! Na fight? Man no fit greet you?

DETIBA. Go away. Go and do your spying somewhere else.

WARDER. Me? Spy? To God who make me . . . !

EMUKE. Shurrup! Make you no take God name play for this place you hear? No to you go report to security say the Superintendent dey do favouritism for some detainees?

WARDER. I swear, not to me o. Wetin me I get with Security? Who tell you that kind 'tory?

DETIBA. Word gets around in this place, don't you worry. We were warned against you.

WARDER. Who warn you? You see my face before?

DETIBA. Yes. Someone pointed you out as we passed your morning parade.

WARDER. Anybody wey accuse me for that kind ting, God no go make in own better. I swear . . .

EMUKE. And if na true dem accuse you, wetin make God do you?

WARDER. Make I die for dis useless job! Make all my family no prosper for den life.

DETIBA *and* EMUKE *look up at each other; they resolve some doubt.*

DETIBA. He'll do, Mr Domingo.

EMUKE. Yes, you fit risk am.

WARDER (*at first puzzled, then a slow grin*). O-oh-oh, na test you dey test me.

DETIBA. What's your name?

WARDER. Amidu.

DETIBA (*offering him a packet*). Do you smoke?

WARDER (*quick look up and down passage*). I go take one for later.

DETIBA. Take more than one.

DETIBA *shakes several cigarettes into* WARDER's *hand.* WARDER *stuffs them into his pocket.*

WARDER. Thank you, thank you sirs. Ah, you disturb me well well before. Me? Wetin I dey get from government I go spy for them?

DETIBA. We had to be sure. Our friend here needs courier service. He wants to send a letter.

WARDER. Things hard small o. They give us all kind of checks nowadays. Coming in, going out, even spot checks. It's no joke.

DETIBA. He's willing to pay.

MIGUEL. It's just a letter. (*Brings out an envelope.*) The address is on it. Everybody knows the house.

WARDER (*recognising the address, he looks at* DOMINGO *with some awe*). O-oh, na you be the . . .

MIGUEL. Make sure you give it to her, in person. It's my mother.

WARDER. I go bring reply?

MIGUEL. There'll be no need. But hand it to her personally. Don't give it to anyone else.

WARDER. If I no meet her nko?* I fit go back any time you want.

MIGUEL. You'll meet her all right. She doesn't leave the house – except on Saturday mornings. Any other time of day, you'll find her at home. And she'll make it worth your while.

EMUKE. You hear that, Mr Postmaster General.

WARDER. You sure say you no wan' make she send something? I sure say I can manage bring you anything

*'Nko?' means 'what then?'

you want. Anything at all. Whether na food or drink or money, just write am for note.

MIGUEL. No, I'm afraid you can't bring me the only thing I want. But it doesn't matter. Soon we won't be needing anything.

EMUKE *glances at him uneasily.* DETIBA *also, but he shrugs it off.*

WARDER. Look, you people, I no know if you get interest but er . . . (*Nods towards* MIGUEL.) . . . 'e look like say you get the means to do something for yourselves (*he digs into his pocket and brings out a small, oval object, bound tightly in white leather and black thread.*)

DETIBA. What is that?

WARDER. You hear of bandufu before?

DETIBA. Ban-du . . . Oh yes, bandufu. Is that what that is?

EMUKE. Wetin be bandufu?

WARDER. Some people no believe am but make a tell you, I done see the thing wey bandufu fit do. I take my own very eyes see am. These oyinbo people can talk any nonsense they want but blackman power dey where 'e day.

EMUKE. Chineke God! You no fit answer simple question? Wetin be bandufu?

DETIBA. I'll tell you. It's supposed to make you invisible. Disappear. Vanish into thin air.

EMUKE. Sho? (*Reaches out his hand through the bars.*)

WARDER. You get interest or not?

DETIBA. Go away. Emuke, don't you fall for that nonsense.

EMUKE. No? Me I get interest, why not?

DETIBA. It's a swindle. These people just use it to make money.

WARDER. I tell you two prisoner vanish before my very eyes. And na dis very bandufu do am.

EMUKE. Tell me how 'e dey work.

WARDER. If you get interest, make we talk business first.

DETIBA. What did I tell you? It's business first and last.

EMUKE. Wait small. Tell me how dis 'ting dey work.

DETIBA *throws up his hands in despair.*

WARDER. 'E get certain ting wey you go say, that all. You tie the bandufu for your waist, or put am somewhere it must touch your body. Then, you recite the incantation. Very short. You call the name of any ancestor you get wey done die, then your own name – if you get oriki, you call all your oriki. Then finally, the place where you wan' land. Dat one very important because, if you no tell dis medicine where it must take you, 'e fit land you for inside jungle or overseas, or even back inside your enemy hand.

EMUKE. How much 'e go cost?

DETIBA. Emuke!

EMUKE. Look my friend, wetin we go take money do for de place where tribunal wan' send us. Abi bandufu dey work over dere? 'E fit bring me back to this world?

WARDER. Na proper sense you dey talk. But as for cost, you know this kin' medicine must cost. All de ingredients wey dey inside, including the hair from private part of person wey just die. . . .

EMUKE. Why you like dey talk so much? I say how much?

WARDER. Twelve kilos.

DETIBA. What! You bloody fraud!

WARDER. My friend, make a tell you about this very one. The babalawo wey make am, 'e done finish de main ting since three months. But the power no complete because 'e no get that last ingredient wey I mention.

EMUKE. You mean the hair from private part?

WARDER. That's right. Every time prisoner die, I no get lucky to dey for duty, and na me only this babalawo come trust. In any case de other warders, den dey fear de man too much.

DETIBA. Ooh. So the babalawo is inside this prison?

WARDER. Na in a dey tell you! 'E dey for lunatic cell.

EMUKE. Kai. Na crazeman medicine you wan' sell me?

WARDER. No, not to say 'e craze. But the power wey 'e dey take make dis kin' medicine 'e dey turn in head. When dat happen, nobody fit go near am. Na me one den go call.

DETIBA. So where did this vital hair come from?

WARDER (*pointing*). General cell. One prisoner die there day before yesterday. As luck be, na me dey for duty, so I unlock the babalawo make 'e come shave in pubic hair, before I make official report. The hair wey lef', 'e fit make two more, so if all of una want. . . .

EMUKE (*eagerly*). You see. De power go still fresh, no be so?

DETIBA. Emuke, don't be such a fool!

WARDER. I'm telling you. Is very lucky. Since that babalawo dey prison, na only four bandufu 'e fit make. And na me dey look for customer for am. I tell you, two prisoner wey use the medicine, dem vanish commot prison. Till today nobody fit find dem. Nobody. One na rapist wey get ten years, de other na counterfeit money maker wey den give fifteen years.

DETIBA. You are worse than a rapist. You are both necrophiliac and grave-robber. But I hope the other one paid you in counterfeit money.

EMUKE (*despondently*). But wissai me a go get twelve thousand, even for counterfeit notes?

WARDER (*gestures to* MIGUEL). 'E fit lend you. If 'e just add small note for this letter, in mama go send de money.

DETIBA. You're betting on the wrong horse. You think someone like him believes in that kind of rubbish?

EMUKE. No to im go use am. Na me wan try de ting.

WARDER. Look, inspection time done near. Make up your mind quick quick or I must go try somebody else.

EMUKE *hesitates. Then approaches* MIGUEL.

EMUKE. Er . . . Mr Domingo . . . ?

MIGUEL *turns round slowly, the ghost of a grin on his face. He digs his hand under his trouser waistband and extracts an object identical to the* WARDER's.

MIGUEL. Why don't you try mine Emuke? It's already paid for, and as you see, it has never been used.

DETIBA. You? You mean you . . .

MIGUEL. A family friend slipped it to me on our fateful day in court. (*He takes out a piece of paper, wraps the object in it.*) The incantation is written there.

DETIBA. Did you try it?

MIGUEL. I never would have thought I would. I always laughed at such things but, after that sentencing . . . it's amazing what desperation does to you. (*Throws it to* EMUKE.) Here. Maybe it will work for you.

DETIBA (*breaks into a chuckle*). Better luck elsewhere my friend. Try one of the ex-Ministers . . .

WARDER (*gives a prolonged hiss, then flings* DOMINGO's *letter on the cell floor*). Some people dey, wey even heaven no fit help. Ye-ye people!

The spot traverses stage to reveal the general cell where the STUDENT's *curriculum vitae is still in progress.*

General cell. HYACINTH's *'Cabinet' surround the* STUDENT *as if he is the centre of an interrogation.*

COMMANDANT. You are sure you are not trying to play tough guy? You actually went back?

STUDENT. I was desperate for a fix. And I thought they would come after me right away. The Wing Commander carried a gun for all I knew. People get shot all the time in that part of the city, no questions asked.

NUMBER 2. And you sneaked back into the house? Wonderful boy!

STUDENT. It was the safest place to hide and I knew the house inside out. I told you, I was his trusted courier. He would send me to go and take out thousands from under his bed or other hiding-places.

NUMBER 2. Before you caught the habit.

STUDENT. Yes, that was the start of my disaster. He used to fence for us – that's how I got to know him. We stole valuables from our parents' colleagues while our own friends would rob our parents. We left the door open for one another, it was easy. Sebe would buy the goods from us. Stereos, jewellery, even motor tyres and spare parts. Then one day he asked me if I would like to earn some really big money . . . well, from then on, it was one thing leading to another. We got on well. He treated me like a son.

COMMANDANT. Security!

DIRECTOR. Yes Commandant.

COMMANDANT. What do you think?

DIRECTOR. I must confess I am most impressed. The boy thinks like a soldier. First he hides in what seems the most dangerous place. Then he commits a slight misdemeanour to get himself arrested and thrown in gaol – for his own safety.

General nods and noises of approval.

COMMANDANT. Yes, but the question is, what is he worth? How much do you think Sebe will pay if we let him know the boy is here? And that we have people here ready to do the job for him.

HOME. Chief, the young man has thrown himself on our protection.

COMMANDANT. A junkie! Dope addict!

NUMBER 2. Ex.

COMMANDANT. Okay, ex. He had no choice but to kick the habit in here. What you can't maintain indoors you kick out of doors – big deal! The point is, what's the deal? Where does Amaroko come in? If we're going to cross Sebe Irawe over this stray dog, what's in it for us?

HOME. Maybe his CV will tell us.

INFORMATION. Let's vote on it Commandant. I don't like getting on the wrong side of Sebe. We're in here; he is out. He can make things hot for us.

HOME. Not forgetting that he's got the Air Force working for him.

DIRECTOR. I doubt if it will come to the vote, Commandant.

COMMANDANT. No? (*Grins.*) Securico himself! I think the Major has detected something we've all missed.

DIRECTOR. I believe so. Why should he have revealed so much? Why take the risk? (*He walks up to the* STUDENT.) You know where the missing goods are, don't you?

STUDENT (*nods*). Yes, I do. I was watching Sebe very closely.

Excited reactions.

COMMANDANT. See? The boy is devious. Devious! He's been holding out on us.

INFORMATION. You are real sneaky for your age, sonny. Putting us through all those appetizers but you left out the really juicy part.

STUDENT. It's in the final episode.

DIRECTOR. I told you. He's sharp.

COMMANDANT. It's blackmail.

STUDENT. No, it's bargaining. Do we have a deal or not?

INFORMATION. I still say let's vote on it. Sebe . . .

COMMANDANT. Shut up! Who is Sebe? When did his authority extend to Amaroko? I am in command here.

NUMBER 2. Vote, vote, vote! You think we're running a democracy here?

HOME. Those politicians have messed up his brain. I've told the Superintendent he should always put them in a separate cell. They come here and contaminate decent criminals – that's the result.

COMMANDANT. You know what the value of fifty kilos of cocaine comes to? And you start whining about vote or no vote. Nonsense! Take your places for the real thing! Studentco, we talk business later, you and I.

DIRECTOR. Count me in; you'll need my expertise.

HYACINTH *nods. Signals to the* SERGEANT-MAJOR.

SERGEANT-MAJOR. Places everyone!

They scramble 'offstage', leaving HYACINTH *and* NUMBER 2 *in their last positions. They sing the last verse of 'Diplomatic Bag'.*

WING COMMANDER (*sighs*). Those were kindergarten days, Chief. Peanut pickings. This is our introduction into the Big League, and if we don't act big, we shall lose our membership.

SEBE (*wringing his hands*). I know, I know. It worries me night and day.

WING COMMANDER. Fifty kilograms of prime grade cocaine is not chicken feed. Countries have gone to war for less.

SEBE. Don't we know it, Commander, don't we know it? If my memory serves me right, you soldiers have even declared war against one another over football. Common football!

WING COMMANDER. Who did?

SEBE. You remember – those a-rhumba-styley countries in Latin America, about the size of my backyard vegetable patch – yes, one of them was Honduras . . .

WING COMMANDER. And so? What has football got to do with our own matter? I am talking about big league and you start talking football league.

SEBE. Nothing Commander, nothing. I was simply agreeing with you.

A brief silence, during which the WING COMMANDER *eyes* SEBE *with deep suspicion.*

WING COMMANDER. You know, Sebe, I get this feeling that you are making fun of me.

SEBE. Me? God forbid! My friend, why should such a thing cross your mind. This is a matter of life and death.

WING COMMANDER (*with rising fury*). I spend the entire morning telling you that you and your men are slow, and you start talking of some banana republics which begin by shooting football and end up shooting bullets. Are we playing games? Or your men? Somebody is playing games somewhere, and in a matter that touches my honour. My honour is at stake!

SEBE. Cool down Commander . . .

WING COMMANDER. The operation was masterminded by the very cream of the ruling junta. Nobody knew of the special bag in that shipment in this country except myself – and you.

SEBE (*backing away*). Ah, no, no, not at all my dear partner. All you told me was to prepare myself for something big, that was all. What it was, when it would come, how it would come . . . Commander, for all I knew it could be guns and ammunition for another coup.

WING COMMANDER. Don't talk rot!

SEBE. Or for sale or hire to armed robbers. Commander, all I am saying is that I knew nothing. It could have been gold. Or diamonds. Or contraband like ivory tusks – I am just a conduit pipe Commander, I have never pretended to be anything else.

WING COMMANDER. My arrangements were through. I never leave anything to chance – never! I assigned a top officer to clear the consignment and transfer it to the armoury. The formal presentation by the Pakistani Ambassador was to await my arrival – I made sure of that. The letter of friendship from President Zia is right here, in my briefcase. Here, take a look at it . . . (*He fumbles with the lock of his attaché-case, opens it and flourishes the letter.*) Take a look! That is the presidential seal . . .

SEBE. Commander, I know, I know . . .

WING COMMANDER. I just want you to understand that nothing, absolutely nothing was left to chance. Nobody could touch any part of that consignment before I arrived with this letter.

SEBE. The top officer who did the clearing . . . ?

WING COMMANDER (*irritably*). Except him of course. Naturally. And he knew nothing of the special bag. His job was simply to clear a high-security shipment and store it in the armoury! But the pirates got there before him, the very night the ship berthed.

SEBE. The harm is done Commander. What we must think of is how to undo it.

WING COMMANDER. Sebe, you hold the key to this entire business. Put pressure on your people!

SEBE. Commander, please. Ask around. I am a middleman. I don't launch pirates against sea-going vessels. Violence is alien to my temperament.

WING COMMANDER. No one is accusing you, but nearly all the underworld report here, sooner or later.

SEBE. I am only a link in the chain Commander. A small man.

They hold each other's eyes for moments. The WING COMMANDER *is barely containing his rage.* SEBE *wears a sardonic smile.*

WING COMMANDER. Just remember what is at stake. For me. And for you. We military stick together, remember that. We may settle scores among ourselves from time to time, even bloodily, but in the end, we close ranks. When we do . . .

SEBE. . . . we bloody civilians become the scapegoats.

WING COMMANDER. I'm glad you know that.

SEBE. Or perhaps, to be more accurate, we provide the scapegoats. Expendables. But people like us, Commander, continue with business as usual.

WING COMMANDER. Not always. Sometimes, the stakes are so big we cannot accept just any scrawny scapegoat. That's when we go for the fatted calf. Then, nobody remains immune. Nobody.

SEBE (*sighs deeply*). I understand, Chief. I understand you only too well.

WING COMMANDER. I need results Sebe. I need results, fast! My partners are impatient and my standing is at stake. I dare not return without something concrete to report, and of course I cannot remain here for ever. My course still has three months to go – if I stay too long I shall run out of excuses. Once the handing-over ceremony is over . . .

SEBE. You can always mount a coup.

WING COMMANDER (*looking round wildly*). Don't say that again! I don't find it funny.

SEBE. It's not meant to be funny. It is accepted cover-up practice.

WING COMMANDER. Not here in Nigeria.

SEBE. Who knows if it may yet happen. But I was thinking of Uganda as a matter of fact. Didn't the one and only Idi Amin stage his coup over his ivory and diamonds smuggling? (*Conspiratorially.*) They say Obote was about to put him on trial when he struck.

WING COMMANDER (*grimly*). Yes, quite a man of current affairs, we know.

SEBE. Business, my friend, business. We try to keep abreast of world affairs. One doesn't get to know the forest by climbing only the trees in his village. The learning process is what keeps us afloat and alive, Commander.

WING COMMANDER. Yes, staying alive. That's very important. Let's not forget that, Chief.

SEBE (*casting a furtive look at the* WING COM-MANDER). May I make a suggestion Chief?

WING COMMANDER. What now?

SEBE. A suggestion. Something I have just thought of.

WING COMMANDER. Well, let's hear it.

SEBE. You see, it seems to me that you have not really tapped all the resources at your disposal. I mean, you are after all a member of the Ruling Council.

WING COMMANDER. What are you getting at?

SEBE. Use that resource.

WING COMMANDER. Of course, I intend to.

SEBE. No, I can tell you haven't thought of this – get the
Council to declare a State of Emergency.

WING COMMANDER. A what?

SEBE. A State of Emergency.

WING COMMANDER. You must be mad.

SEBE. Am I?

WING COMMANDER. Declare a State of Emergency! On
what grounds?

SEBE. Any excuse will do. Close all the borders. Tighten up
Customs. Decree a stop-and-search authorisation for all
the uniformed services. Anywhere, anytime, night and
day or – wait! That's it! Make it a crackdown on drugs,
special campaign. Round up all known drug-users and
pushers. No exception. Detain suspects without trial.
Even the petty ones. When you squeeze the belle tight, the
fart go commot.

WING COMMANDER. You mean, actually admit that a
consignment is missing?

SEBE. No, no, no Commander. Simply launch a special
campaign – it may even bring you extra aid from World
Health Organisation. Make it the next stage of the battle
against indiscipline, emphasis on drug abuse. Commander, don't tell me you can't sell such a brilliant,
straightforward clean-up exercise to your Ruling Council.

WING COMMANDER (*gives it serious thought*). It's a
sellable idea.

SEBE. More than sellable. It is buyable. We squeeze the
users, squeeze the pushers, squeeze the pirates who did
the actual hijacking – somewhere along the line someone
will break and tell us just who is sitting on a hundred
million US dollars. My spies will easily find out who is
panicking and then you can pounce!

WING COMMANDER. It may work. It may work.

SEBE. It will work. It has to. It is a national undertaking,

but in true military style. No voice will be raised in
opposition.

WING COMMANDER (*paces thoughtfully*). It should
work. I think I know how to present it to the Ruling
Council.

SEBE. Sway them Commander, sway them. I know you can
do it. Get them to seal up the entire country tighter than a
virgin's you-know-what. Give us the old stop-and-search
routine. Search, but not destroy!

WING COMMANDER (*giggling*). After all, the missing
item is State property.

SEBE. So it is, so it is.

WING COMMANDER. Well then, it deserves State mobil-
isation.

SEBE. That's the spirit, my Commander. It's a state
assignment . . .

WING COMMANDER. For a State consignment.

Together: Song of State Assignment

State assignment
For State consignment
State machinery
For State chicanery
Scorched earth strategy
Will provoke the allergy
To expose that very hidden
Commodity forbidden

Don't mess with the military
Or we'll write your obituary
Underworld and over-brass
No one dare embarrass
Power, the pure commodity
To which our little ditty

Is for ever consecrated
Don't ignore or underrate it

State machinery
For State chicanery
Let who can resolve the riddle
How we guarantee the fiddle
Mum's the word among the ranks
Mum's the word in foreign banks
When State assignments coincide
With State consignments far and wide.

WING COMMANDER. You know something else?

SEBE. What is that, dear partner?

WING COMMANDER. We'll make it retroactive.

SEBE. You will make what retroactive?

WING COMMANDER. The campaign of course. The Law, the Decree, the penalties. It will show we mean business. And anyway, that's our style. That's how people recognize who's in charge. That's the difference between you and us. Civilians can only operate in linear time. We go backwards and forwards at will.

SEBE. And in circles. Brilliant! Don't we know it? Your patron god is Esu (*Confidentially.*) And let me tell you, we must not neglect the little fellow.

WING COMMANDER. Who? What little fellow?

SEBE. Esu. Small but potent. (*Unveils his Esu shrine.*) You know his oriki don't you? He throws a stone today and it kills a man last week. That retroactive twist is just the kind of idea he inspires in men of action.

WING COMMANDER. Look, Sebe, you stick to your superstitions. I will take care of practical measures.

SEBE. Practical measures, Commander, practical measures? As we are talking here, do you know how many

different shrines are receiving sacrifices from our opponents to buy protection for the missing goods? Do you
know how many bodies will be found with all their vital
organs missing? That missing bag itself is almost a deity
that must be propitiated. It has become a god in its own
right.

WING COMMANDER. Sure, sure. As I said, stick to your
own plans . . .

SEBE. Commander, I will surely vex with you. You people,
you think you know everything. Armed robbers know
better. They know what they must do before an operation,
and I am telling you Commander, they can proof themselves against your bullets . . .

WING COMMANDER. We've heard that often enough,
but they end up in the morgue just the same.

SEBE. The ones who didn't choose the right experts. There
are doctors and doctors Commander, just as there are
soldiers and soldiers.

WING COMMANDER. That's it exactly. Some soldiers
believe in all that stuff. I am not one of them.

SEBE. If I could do it all by myself, I wouldn't bother you.
But you are the principal. The whole thing began with
you. When I visit the major crossroads at midnight to put
down the calabash, and Esu asks me, where is the
principal petitioner, what will I say? The little man will
simply laugh, eat the sacrifice and attend to more serious
people.

WING COMMANDER. You really believe all that rubbish?

SEBE. My friend, do as I say. Come with me. What are we
trying to do if not to seal up all the roads so this juicy
mouse does not escape? We are dealing with the crossroads, so . . . yes, tell me, doesn't the Bible itself say —
render unto Caesar what is Caesar's and unto God what is

God's? It's the same thing. In any case what is wrong with
a little insurance? Commander, look at me! Just look at
me! Muslim, Christian, Animist, Bhuddist, Aborisa —
now that combination is what you call — practical measures. Insurance policies. Maybe if you had thought of
invoking Olokun, guardian of the seas, the pirates would
have been drowned while attempting the hijack. (*He
unveils several shrines while speaking.*)

WING COMMANDER (*faltering.*) This is so much nonsense. . . .

SEBE. Well, humour me. Say you're doing it for Sebe. You
are doing it for your business partner, for your friend, to
boost his confidence. I will even provide you the white
cloth to wear, and black cap . . .

WING COMMANDER. White cloth! Black cap?

SEBE. Leave the details to me. In one hour, it will all be
over. Just remember that those on the other side are not
sitting down idly. They are mobilising all the powers, and
we must neutralise them. What time do you finish your
Council meeting?

WING COMMANDER. Well, sometimes it goes on till
midnight. And if I am to propose these new measures and
get them through . . .

SEBE. Come here straight after the meeting. Four crossroads, that's more than enough. It won't take more than
one hour to do the rounds. I have my own priest and
shrine for every single deity. I don't broadcast my piety,
but I am always prepared.

WING COMMANDER. This whole thing is crazy.

SEBE. The people who did this thing to us, they want to
prosper, not so? We also want to prosper. Even if I don't
know them yet, I know their habits. I know exactly what
they will do, what they are doing. If I may just adapt our
ancient saying to the circumstances — if everybody makes

fun of someone, saying that the fellow is acting crazy, and yet we see that fellow prospering, doing well, being successful, then isn't it time we also sipped a little of the potion of insanity?

WING COMMANDER (*grinning*). You know how to give a twist to everything.

SEBE. I am a practical man, Commander. I keep a toe in every shrine and a finger in every business pie. Your man is Esu, but you are going more modern. Esu only throws stones, you, you fire bullets. But Esu is broadminded, don't worry. He won't be resentful of your prowess – that is, as long as we give him his due. This exercise enh, you'll see, when you fire a bullet today, it will have hit its target long before you ever took over government. Now that is real power for you.

WING COMMANDER (*rapt in the prospect*). You know, the power to act backwards in time . . .

SEBE. And it was all your own idea! Didn't I say it? You people are trained to think big.

WING COMMANDER. I shall spin a net with a small mesh. Even the sprats cannot escape it.

SEBE. When you cast that net, Commander, even the fishes that swam through those waters the year before will be snared. There is no escape for anyone, big or small.

WING COMMANDER. It's the ultimate time-machine. When we launch it . . .

SEBE. All it requires is libation. A little midnight libation, just to be on the good side of the little man.

WING COMMANDER. Lubrication, not libation. A trusty sub-machine gun well lubricated, that's all it takes to bring things back under control.

SEBE. SMG or SMOG – the difference is 'O'. (*Shapes his fingers to form an 'O'*.) Zero.

WING COMMANDER. SMOG?

SEBE. Save me O God. – Libation, prayers, offerings – to whichever powers you choose.

WING COMMANDER. You are impossible, Sebe.

SEBE. You keep saying that, my friend. Why? I am possible. I am the only possible type of businessman in this country.

WING COMMANDER. Well, for me, the sub-machine gun guarantees the time-machine. But, all right, I'll humour you.

SEBE. It's ready for launching then. Move it against everything in our way. It's war-time Wing Commander. It's a moral crusade – slackness, rigidity, forgery, connery, venery, revelry, smuggling, ogling, laziness, eagerness, apathy, telepathy, intolerance, permissiveness, academia, kleptomania, cultism, nepotism, nudity, drunkenness, superstition, godlessness, loitering, muttering, rioting, malingering, rumour-mongering . . .

Rap of the Military Time-Machine:

The prisoners stomp on stage in a variety of military cast-offs, some with gas masks – half-face with goggles – several with 'Tyson' crew-cuts, cavorting in 'rap' motions. They go through their contortions in precision drill, chanting the chorus in the 'rap-recitativo' mode. WING COMMANDER *takes the solo, later joined by* SEBE *who hugs himself with delight and dances with approval as the* WING COMMANDER *develops his campaign of 'reforms'.*

CHORUS.
  I got you in a trap
    on the time-machine
  If you don't take the rap
    I cannot preen

Myself as Mr Clean
  now that makes me mean
To long you've been
  on the money scene.
While the fact of my being,
  is – my pocket's lean
I ain't worth a bean
  to a sweet sixteen
I ain't been seen
  with no beauty queen
Who says I ain't keen.
  on pastures green?
So you've got a trip coming
  on the time-machine
Time you went roaming
  in a change of scene.

WING COMMANDER.
We shan't be confined
  just to future time
Retribution shall fall
  on any previous crime
Of refining, sniffing
  tasting or injecting
Buying, retailing,
  distributing, inspecting
(Except of course
  by authorized agents)
Liquid, or solid, or
  powdery halucinogens.
To expedite this mission
  we hereby erect
A military tribunal
  with immediate effect

Its powers shall be subject
   to no confines
No bail shall be granted
   no option of fines
No option of prison
   or community service
No right of appeal
   no delaying device.
CHORUS.
   I got you in a trap (*Etc.*)
WING COMMANDER.
Every offender shall be
   guilty as charged
Acquittal shall mean
   conditionally discharged
Surrender of passport
   report every morning
To the nearest police
   or else keep running
As for fugitive suspects
   seize every spouse
And children as hostage
   place a price on the louse
From the tiniest of doses
   to wholesale vendor
Habitual user or
   first-time offender
Laundering of earnings
   from drug operation
Shall incur something worse
   than life incarceration
It's forfeit of life
   by firing squad
And forfeit of property

at home or abroad
Be it liquid asset
    or landed estate
And any other forfeiture
    as decided by the State.
CHORUS.
I got you in a trap (*Etc*.)
WING COMMANDER.
We're going to clean up
    every damned city
Without fear or favour
    or any shred of pity
And those who think
    there's refuge in the village
Will find we're all set
    for rural life pillage
So bring out your skeletons
    open up your closets
Or we'll dig them out
    on the tips of rusty bayonets
All your dens of decadence
    in affluent suburbs
Are going to feel the weight
    of military curbs
So pull up your socks
-    the Army's now in charge
Shape up or ship out
    the drill-major's at large
We're building a new nation
    cleaning out the rot
Ending your civilian torpor
    striking while it's hot
And remember we're the breed
    whose bullets, fired the day before

Hit their mark the previous year
    and penetrate your door.

CHORUS.
    I got you in a trap (*Etc.*)

WING COMMANDER.
    There's too much thinking going on
      we'll put an end to it
    We've had enough of dissidents
      they must conform or quit
    We're rooting for the radicals
      rooting them out
    There ain't room for them and us
      We're puttng them to rout
    Pay attention to my rap
      or you going to take the rap
    For things you think you never thought
      but which fit your mental map.

CHORUS.
    I got you in a trap (*Etc.*)

Next to invade the platform is a skimpy figure clad only in even skimpier underpants, blowing an outsize saxophone. He is followed by female dancers doing a 'shinamanic' dance to the tune of 'Zombie'. The earlier group retreat. The WING COMMANDER *stares aghast, recovers, and breaks into maniacal laughter. His voice overwhelms the music of the intruders, while the first group resume their motions with greater vigour.*

WING COMMANDER.
    *Chief Kalakuta priest
      we've got him in our sights

*See p. 105

The way we deal with mavericks
    he'll scream for human rights
So his club was burnt to cinders
    The culprit was unknown
Accidents do happen
    the affair was overblown
How fairer could we be?
    We set up judicial probes
The learned judge was neutral
    correct in legal robes
This cat's mother fixated
    why the obsessive worry?
She fell out of the window
    soldiers don't say 'sorry'
Does he let her rest in peace?
    He tries to deposit
Her coffin on our doorstep
    – well, that really does it!
Resurrect her if you can,
    build another Kalakut'
You'll learn the brutal truth
    of power, Mr Cool-and-Cute!

CHORUS.
    You're got a trip coming
        on the time – machine
    Time you went roaming
        in a change of scene.

WING COMMANDER.
    He thought we'd chase him smoking pot;
        no, foreign currency
    Was where we chose to nail his arse
        – no clemency!

CHORUS.
    I got you in a trap. (*Etc.*)

As the saxophonist is overwhelmed, manacled and encased in prison clothes, his entourage disappear one after the other.

WING COMMANDER.
Lock him up! Yap him
enough years to scare 'im
Muffle up his Afro-beat and
scatter wide his harem
Let him file for bankruptcy,
silence his cacophony
No air-wave may vibrate
except to army symphony.
CHORUS.
You're got a trip coming
on the time-machine
Time you went roaming
in a change of scene.
WING COMMANDER.
This nation is caught
in a moral crisis
The road shall be hard
to dis'plinary bliss
This new broom's set to sweep
with all its strands of steel
No taking 'No' for answer
all shoulders to the wheel
All suggestive images are
banned from stage and journals
The decadence of modern tastes
is banished from our portals
It's back to fundamentalism
strict moralistic values

National flag, national pledge
public rallies and rulers' statues.
CHORUS.
I've got you in a trap (*Etc.*)

Light comes on in cell 'C'.

LOUDSPEAKER. BAI Culture is for you, and You! Do
not not exempt yourself from the Battle Against Indiscipline. Tighten your belt. Redemption may be sooner than
you think. No citizen is beyond redemption. Cultivate
vigilance. Report anything suspicious. Play a role in
preserving our sovereign integrity. Subversion can sprout
in the unlikeliest places – root it out! Fight the drug
menace. Drug dealers are national saboteurs – sniff them
out! Root them out! Forward with BAI, the vanguard of
our national redemption.

MIGUEL (*shakes his head, doleful*). I would have thought
that in prison at least, one would be spared this obscene
litany.

DETIBA. How can? Think of the number of captive
audience behind bars.

MIGUEL. Do they really believe that any inmate . . . I
mean, do they really think they can make citizens and
patriots with such banalities?

DETIBA. Think of it this way. It's part of the softening up
process. Like being locked up in general cell with those
hardened sadists.

MIGUEL. What?

DETIBA. The beating-up. Don't tell me you've forgotten . . .

MIGUEL. How could I? But . . . that was a mistake. The
Superintendent said so. He apologised.

EMUKE *breaks into laughter.*

DETIBA. All right, let's give the boss himself the benefit of the doubt. But he is not the one who interracts daily with inmates. Those warders make the rules. Or rather, they break the rules and replace them with a system of their own. It's part of the general extortion racket. The hard core prisoners soften you up, they rush in and rescue you. You feel eternally grateful.

MIGUEL. Are you saying you've been through it before?

DETIBA. It wasn't as rough as yours but, everybody goes through some form of initiation. You see, you are rich, you are well known. You have contacts. You would be expected to know your rights and to stand up for them. So, they had to let you know the rules are different here.

EMUKE. Yeah. You be grammar people. Na you cause the extra sufferment wey me and Detiba suffer. Look, if to say you no came back, they no even go fit sentence we. All the newspapers go cry out say dem sentence small fry while big fish done escape.

MIGUEL. Nonsense! You don't really believe that.

EMUKE. Believe o or no believe o, I still no sabbe why you come back for that court.

MIGUEL. It's nothing you'll understand. Call it fate if you like – I am here, like you, awaiting death. (*Bitter laugh*.) Miguel Omowale Domingo, the colonial aristocrat, I think one sneering journalist called me. Business yuppy of the year – that was two years ago I think. But always the favourite media gossip socialite, lionised in any social watering-hole.

EMUKE. Yeah. And now?

MIGUEL. Caged. From all-night dancing to the dance of death.

An uncomfortable pause.

DETIBA. Tell me, that is, if you want to. Emuke and I, well, we were actually caught with the stuff. But you . . . I mean, were you framed?

MIGUEL (*quietly*). In business these days, you walk a tightrope. That's if you really want to make it. Otherwise you're just a noisy monkey with the rest of the herd. You make enemies and . . . well, hired assassins or judicial butchers, what's the difference? Business is just another circus. You have the clowns, and you have the high-risk performers.

DETIBA. So, returning to face trial when you were free on bail – was that part of the risk-taking?

MIGUEL. I've told you, there is also that element of fate, or whatever you choose to call it.

EMUKE *steps forward impatiently and begins the song 'Farewell, Social Lion' with its chorus.* DETIBA *joins in with the main verses. He sings with a tinge of pathos while* EMUKE's *chorus is aggressive and impatient.*

EMUKE (*Chorus*).
   Yes, yes, talk all the grammar you want
   But you came back like a fool
   Like a pig to the slaughter.
DETIBA.
   You're right, it's a circus and you're doing your stunt
   Half-way across the tension wire, the champion starts to drool
   The safety net has vanished; your soul turns to water.
EMUKE *Chorus*.
DETIBA.
   Monarch with the coiffured mane, your dreaded claws are blunt

You're just a well-trained lion crouching on his stool
Jumping to the whipcrack of the spangled circus master.

EMUKE. *Chorus.*

DETIBA.

Oh brave Mr Lion, welcome from the hunt
Your poise is so stately, your bearing is so cool
Is your cage quite cosy or would you like something softer!

EMUKE. *Chorus.*

DETIBA.

To turn your back on danger is an option you have shunned
A *preux chevalier*, you never break a rule
Neither is this world, nor in the life hereafter.

MIGUEL.

The life hereafter?

EMUKE.

Yes, yes, talk the grammar you want

MIGUEL.

The life hereafter?

EMUKE.

You come back like a fool

MIGUEL.

The life hereafter?

EMUKE.

Like a pig to de slaughter

DETIBA.

It ends in a staccato, a whimper or a grunt
We'll walk with some bravado, then briefly spurt a pool
Of the purple stuff, and ascend the heavenly rafter.

MIGUEL.

Life is a rotter

DETIBA and EMUKE.

Talk the grammar you want

MIGUEL.

Power is even rottener

DETIBA and EMUKE.
  You come back like a fool
MIGUEL.
  But rottener than rottenest
DETIBA and EMUKE.
  Like a pig to de slaughter
MIGUEL.
  Is power that makes the breaks
DETIBA and EMUKE.
  That makes the breaks
ALL.
  The very rule it makes and breaks
  It makes and breaks.

A pause. Then a pair of boots along the corridor. Officer
AREMU *appears and stops at the cell door.*

AREMU. Mr Domingo, the Superintendent wanted you to
  see this. (*Passes a newspaper to him.*) There is something
  in there to cheer you up. Everybody is speaking up against
  the sentence.

All three rush to the cell door, DOMINGO *is handed the*
paper.

EMUKE. Wetin den dey talk? Wetin?
DETIBA. Can't you find it? What page is it?
AREMU. It's right there, bottom of the front page. And
  some other statements inside. One of them is from the
  former Chief Justice of the Federation. I'll bring the other
  papers when the boss has finished with them. Everywhere, it's all condemnation, everybody. (*Goes off.*)
MIGUEL (*Reading*). 'National Bar Association condemns
  retroactive laws. The National Bar Association, in a

statement issued at its Apapa Secretariat, has condemned
the practice of enacting laws to deal with offences committed when such laws did not exist . . .'

EMUKE. Wetin former Chief Justice say, na dat one I wan
hear? 'E sentence me one time to four years when 'e still be
common magistrate.

MIGUEL. I'm sure they'll say more or less the same thing.
Here is one from the Roman Catholic Archbishop. 'No
one has a right to take a human life under a law which did
not exist at the time of a presumed offence.' Good,
'presumed'. I'm glad somebody is actually mentioning the
issue of presumption of guilt. If ever there was a clear case
of a verdict dictated from above, against the sheer weight
of evidence . . . ah, here's another – it begins to look like a
ground swell of protests. Even the editorial – hm. Quite
courageous. And the National Students Association . . .
Amnesty, national chapter – oh yes, I'm sure Amnesty
International will take an interest very soon . . . the
Traditional Rulers' Council, they are appealing for
clemency. (*Throws the paper away.*) *Clemency!*

DETIBA. Keep cool, Mr Domingo.

MIGUEL. Clemency! Is that the issue?

DETIBA (*picks up the paper*). Does it matter what they call
it? They all want the same thing, only they're saying it
differently.

MIGUEL. No, it is not the same thing. That is the kind of
language that flatters the bestial egos of such a breed of
rulers. It makes them feel that the world and every living
thing within it is their largesse, from which they dole out
crumbs when they are sated. Clemency! Even a retarded
child must know that the issue is one of justice.

DETIBA. This would be more to your taste then. I've found
the statement of your friend, Emuke.

EMUKE. Wetin 'e talk?

DETIBA (*reading*). 'In his own statement, the former Chief
Justice of the Federation, Sir Tolade Akindero warned
that if the sentence was carried out, it would amount to
judicial murder.' Is that more like it, Mr Domingo?

MIGUEL. Ah, what does it matter anyway? Why do we
deceive ourselves? We're living in a lawless time.

DETIBA. Here's one more. The Crusade for National
Conscience is organising a continuous vigil outside the
prison until the sentence is rescinded.

MIGUEL (*violently*). No!

DETIBA. No? Why not? It all helps to put pressure on the
regime.

MIGUEL. Don't you know who they are?

DETIBA. Not much. I've only heard of them once or twice
– in the papers.

MIGUEL. They are a religious sect who particularly abhor
any form of executions. And they are rather extreme in
their methods. If they hold that vigil and they're ordered
to disperse, they are just as likely to obey as to disobey,
non-violently. This regime will not hesitate to open fire on
them. They are desperate to teach a lesson, teach a lesson,
teach a bloody lesson wherever and however! I don't want
anyone's death on my conscience.

DETIBA. That is really beyond our control, isn't it?

AREMU *returns with a detail of four* OFFICERS,
followed by the SUPERINTENDENT.

SUPERINTENDENT. Everybody get dressed. Mr
Domingo – and you two, same for you. You've been sent
for.

MIGUEL. Who by?

SUPERINTENDENT. We don't know. It's the same men
from the Special Unit that used to fetch your companions
for interrogation. That is, before the trial began.

DETIBA. Interrogation? Are they re-opening the case? Or the Appeal Court? Is the hearing today?

MIGUEL. Today is a Saturday. The courts are not sitting.

They begin dressing, MIGUEL *with deliberate care.*

SUPERINTENDENT. Well, you may be both right and wrong there. You could be appearing before a Review Panel.

MIGUEL. What?

SUPERINTENDENT (*conspiratorial*). I'm not supposed to tell you this, but we received a secret circular yesterday. All offences in your category, including verdicts delivered by the political tribunal, are no longer subject to a decision by the Court of Appeal. The Head of State has taken over their functions. He has created a Review Panel – it's the only kind that would sit on a weekend – I'm only guessing, but I don't see why else they should bother you today.

MIGUEL. Will our lawyers be present? Have they been informed?

SUPERINTENDENT. I'm sorry, I've told you all I know. The usual form for taking you out of prison was brought by the Special Unit. My job is simply to hand you over.

MIGUEL. All right, thank you. (*He looks increasingly thoughtful.*)

SUPERINTENDENT. Actually you don't know how lucky you are to be going away from the premises today. Another set of armed robbers is going to be executed. The stakes are already being set up. Prisoners are confined to their cells – that's the routine – but within an hour the word will go round on the prison grapevine, and then you'd be amazed at the change. The quiet is unearthly, something you feel right under your skin.

MIGUEL. They are shot in the prison yard?

SUPERINTENDENT. No, not inside. On the open

grounds outside the prison. The Military take charge, so
we never know in advance whose turn it is – unless they are
our own prisoners of course. They are brought from other
prisons mostly, taken directly to the grounds outside. All
we get are instructions to prepare so many stakes for such-
and-such o'clock one day or the next. Like this morning.
You're lucky to be out of it. Well, shall we go?

MIGUEL. I'm ready.

At the last moment MIGUEL *hesitates, then drops on the
bed the jacket which he had earlier folded neatly over his
arm. The cell door is unlocked. The three file out of the cell.*

SUPERINTENDENT. I am positive there'll be something
to celebrate by the time you return. We'll hear about it
immediately, you'll see. This junta likes to boast a
reputation for quick decisions.

*They exit. Faces pressed against the bars on other cell
doors watch them go, silently at first. Then they break into
the 'Song of Displaced Moralities'.*

You thought you packed a hell of clout
Super highflyer, super roustabout
When you could have bailed your carcass out
You went and did a turnabout

Your family contacts in high quarters
Would jump at a fart from your hindquarters
When the moment comes, it's rancid waters
You'll piss like our kind from ghetto quarters

What a waste! Sure, you belonged in the upper class
With plenty of sass, but your thinking was crass
Your ethics at war with the common mass
When you piously tore up your safety pass

All blood tastes alike to the bed-bug
Who grudges the landlord of the prison rug
His tariff? Minions or barons of drug
We bleed alike to the homing slug

A man can only talk so much bull, it
Ends when it's time to bite the bullet
Like a feisty rooster, not a cackling pullet
Stage your bravado and retch in your gullet

Cell 'C'.
Enter three TRUSTIES *with spades, buckets and hard scrubbing brushes. They look quickly up and down, enter the vacated cell. One of them lifts his smock and unwinds some tattered pieces of rope which he coils neatly into his bucket. The others are already rummaging through the cell, keeping a watchful eye on the passage.*

FIRST TRUSTY. I don't know why you keep scavenging for those useless bits of rope. Hyacinth will never use them.

SECOND TRUSTY (*testing a piece for strength*). That's only because they don't look reliable. When I find enough of really good pieces . . .

FIRST TRUSTY. Which you know you never will. Bullets have no business sense. They rip the ropes to pieces.

THIRD TRUSTY. You think he'll ever try it?

SECOND TRUSTY. He's sawn off two bars. Swears he's only waiting for the weeds to thin out, then he'll lower himself down and swim across.

FIRST TRUSTY. Weeds my foot! That's only his latest excuse. He sawed up those bars a whole year before his namesakes took over the lagoon. He's scared to leave, that's all. The world outside terrifies him.

THIRD TRUSTY. Not any longer. He is now strongly motivated. He is after Sebe's territory, he and that young student. They are teaming up together. It's big stuff. The rumour is that there is going to be a coup in Lagos underworld. Major Awam is masterminding the takeover.

FIRST TRUSTY. Hyacinth is going to feel very sorry for himself when he gets to know.

THIRD TRUSTY. What?

FIRST TRUSTY. About those three. If he had known, he wouldn't have given them the special reception.

SECOND TRUSTY. Well, he can't blame himself. Who ever heard of such cases being put in general cell?

FIRST TRUSTY *goes through the pockets of* MIGUEL's *jacket. Runs his fingers along the seams.*

FIRST TRUSTY. This must belong to that socialite. The other two never did have more than the clothes on their backs.

SECOND TRUSTY. You think they might get a last-minute reprieve? I mean, it may not even be them . . .

FIRST TRUSTY. It's them all right. Three stakes. And all the hush-hush. And the rush-rush. I hear someone near the top really has it in for them. Or maybe just one of them.

THIRD TRUSTY. Could be woman palava. You never know.

SECOND TRUSTY. Or maybe because of the officer they found murdered yesterday. These soldier people go mad when any of them is touched.

FIRST TRUSTY. Which officer?

SECOND TRUSTY. I overheard the Superintendent and Aremu talking about it. They say he was found on the road in Agege. At the crossroads. His throat was cut. And his vital organs were missing.

FIRST TRUSTY. Are you sure?

SECOND TRUSTY. It was when you followed the detail warder to collect buckets. I was sitting underneath the window and I heard them dicussing the matter. They said his official car was nearby, that was how they could identify him so quickly. Because he wasn't in uniform. He was wearing just a white cloth, a wrapper.

THIRD TRUSTY. A white wrapper?

SECOND TRUSTY. A white wrapper, nothing more. Only it wasn't all that white any more. It was drenched in blood. Oh yes, something also about a black cap.

THIRD TRUSTY. Was it a senior officer?

FIRST TRUSTY. Didn't they mention his name? If he had an official car, he must be very senior.

SECOND TRUSTY. No, they didn't say who it was but it was an Air Force car. Maybe the papers will carry it. Hey, look at this.

He has prised out a twenty-naira note from a shirt collar.

THIRD TRUSTY. That must belong to that Mr Detiba. He and Emuke have been here long enough to know the tricks.

FIRST TRUSTY. There must be more around. Look underneath everything. They may use sellotape to stick it under surfaces.

SECOND TRUSTY. Makes a decent change anyway. When they come from the other prisons, we don't get at the goods until afterwards, and then they are damaged beyond repair.

THIRD TRUSTY. I don't mind the holes so much. Holes can be mended. It's having to clean off all that blood.

FIRST TRUSTY. Stop complaining. You get double rations for a week – that's quite a lot of items to trade with.

THIRD TRUSTY. No it's not. First we set up the stakes,

then we take down the bodies and put them in those cheap coffins. After that we still have to take down the stakes again, scrub them down for the next round.

FIRST TRUSTY. Shut up will you! Do you have to make us do it twice over?

THIRD TRUSTY (*giggling*). Look at him. He's squeamish.

FIRST TRUSTY. I don't want to talk about it, that's all. I do what I have to do and that's enough.

They look at the small pile of items – cigarette lighter, cigarettes, necktie, handkerchief, a packet of biscuits, half a loaf of bread, and other bits of prison rations.

SECOND TRUSTY. Not all that much. I hope the warder won't think we have cheated on him.

FIRST TRUSTY. I overheard Aremu say that the socialite wasn't expecting to have his bail revoked. He went to the Tribunal unprepared.

THIRD TRUSTY. Pity. He would have come in loaded with essential commodities.

SECOND TRUSTY. That warder raised our hopes for nothing.

FIRST TRUSTY. Me too. I thought, this time we'd collect some real goodies.

FIRST TRUSTY (*retrieving the jacket, wistfully*). Think we can get away with this?

SECOND TRUSTY (*shrugs*). It will have to go under water.

FIRST TRUSTY (*folds and squeezes it into the bucket*). It will still fetch something. If we don't give that warder something substantial . . .

THIRD TRUSTY. Remember that detainee who used to fly all his clothes to Hong Kong for laundry? I don't know why I suddenly remember him.

FIRST TRUSTY. It's the silk jacket. It should only go to the dry-cleaners.

SECOND TRUSTY. You think he knew? I mean, leaving this behind . . .

Sound of distant machine-gun fire. The TRUSTIES *freeze. A pause, then three spaced-out single shots. The* TRUSTIES *place their loot in the bucket, begin to gather up their spades, scrubbing brushes and buckets.*

In the background, the prisoners' voices rise in a dirge.

* (*See p. 89*) Chief Kalakuta priest: This refers to the musician Fela Anikulapo-Kuti, a non-conformist musician who was sentenced to a long term of imprisonment, under the military regime depicted in the play, on trumped-up charges of illegal possession of foreign currency. In an earlier brush with yet another military regime, his commune-style home, with studios, known as the 'Kalakuta Republic', was burnt down in broad daylight by soldiers in uniform, with the connivance of the regime. During that raid, his mother was thrown down two floors; she died not long after. Anikulapo-Kuti led a protest march to the State House where he attempted to deliver a symbolic coffin. The Judicial enquiry which was set up to probe the outrage returned the verdict that Kalakuta Republic had been burnt down by 'unknown soldiers'.

A SCOURGE OF HYACINTHS

A Radio Play

A *Scourge of Hyacinths* was first broadcast on BBC Radio 4 on 8 July 1991, with the following cast:

MIGUEL DOMINGO	Hakeem Kae-Kazim
THE MOTHER	Carmen Monroe
AUGUSTINE EMUKE	Tunde Babs
KOLAWOLE DETIBA	Colin McFarlane
CHIME	Nicholas Monu
SUPERINTENDENT	Louis Mahoney
MILITARY VOICE	Ben Onwukwe
NEWSVENDOR	Clarence Smith
ANNOUNCER	Adjoah Andoh

Directed by Richard Wortley

Tramp of footsteps through echoing corridor – five men in a file, but irregular steps. They come raggedly to a stop. Jangle of a bunch of heavy keys. One is selected, inserted in a lock and turned. A heavy steel door swings open. Two of the men enter.

SUPERINTENDENT (*gently*). Yes, you too Mr Domingo. You'll be sharing this cell with your . . . with these two.

The third man enters. The door clangs shut and the key is turned again in the lock. Silence.

A warder will be along before evening with an extra mattress. We are . . . short of beds and other items right now, so you'll just have to manage. I don't have to tell you, the prison is overcrowded. Both the Military Command and Security send everybody in here as if space is no problem. I suppose because we are hemmed in by the lagoon they think this is the most secure prison. Well, you two are already at home here; I am sure you will show Mr Domingo the ropes.

Silence.

I am sorry about how things turned out for you this morning. But I hope you didn't take that sentence seriously. This regime wants to put a scare in people, that's all. If there is anthing we can do for you – under the circumstances – just summon my immediate assistant. I have instructed him to make you as comfortable as possible. All of you. Shall I send you reading material, Mr Domingo?

Silence.

I really am sorry, but you must take your mind off the verdict and try and settle down. Leave the rest to your lawyers. The appeals won't be heard for some time, so there is nothing to do but to put it out of mind. It's hard at first but – we all adjust. Fortunately you are not restricted in any way – well, I mean, not like the politicians. For them it's more and more restrictions every day. No letters, no newspapers, no visitors. In your own case I can use my discretion. You can see I haven't put you in the wing for condemned prisoners – your cell-mates will bear me out – this is the very cell they've occupied while the trial was on. Normally, after a death sentence, we transfer the condemned prisoner to the special wing but, as I said, nobody takes that sentence seriously. Once they've had enough of their little joke, it will be commuted to life. Even less. That's if the Appeal Court doesn't overturn the verdict altogether. Well, I shall drop in on my evening rounds, just to see how you're getting on. Oh yes – Mr Aremu.

WARDER. Yessir.

SUPERINTENDENT. Send them one of the games we seized from the politicians. You see how careful we have to be these days Mr Domingo? Some prison informer sent a report to the secret police that we were giving the politicians preferential treatment. So, orders came that even their pastime – ludo, cards, draughts and other games – everything was to be withdrawn. The warder will bring you what we have and you can make your choice. (*Pause*.) Try and think of the battle as just beginning, Mr Domingo. Same for you two. I shall call in the evening.

The two officers depart, their footsteps fading down the corridor. Silence, except for a soft lapping of water and lagoon sounds. A bed creaks. Footsteps across a concrete floor. Pause.

MIGUEL DOMINGO (*quietly*). So the water hyacinths have spread also to this part of the lagoon. I suppose I ought to feel at home.

Silence.

Again, footsteps across the floor. Metallic noise as if the door has been gently shaken.

MIGUEL. Oh yes; I know this is a prison cell, but it's that court I am not so sure about. The tribunal where the sentence was passed. Was that part of it for real?

Silence.

EMUKE (*bitterly*). You know wetin I think? Even God no fit forgive people like you. Some tings dey, wey God no go forgive, and 'e be like your own be one of them.

DETIBA. Emuke, leave the man alone.

EMUKE. No, lef me! I wan' say it one time and then I no go say anything again. When the man turn up for court today, I no believe my eyes. I say to my self, abi dis man dey craze?

DETIBA. Well, I said the same thing, didn't I? But – what happened has happened. We are all in the same boat.

EMUKE. No, we no dey inside de same boat. Even from before, na inside separate boat we dey. And in own boat better pass we own. We dey inside custody so we no get choice. We must appear before tribunal whether we like am or not. But in own case, 'e get bail. The court grant am bail. He get high connection so they gi'am bail. Then he take in own leg walka inside court – after dey done change decree to capital offence. Dat one, na in I no understand. What kin' sense be dat?

DETIBA. Well, it wasn't we alone. I overheard some reporters – even lawyers – saying the same thing. I don't think I paid much attention to my own case. In any case I already knew the outcome, there was nothing any lawyer could do for me, unless he could bribe enough members of the tribunal. So I passed the time asking myself, why did he come back?

EMUKE. Unless money done pass reach tribunal hand.

DETIBA. Hn-hn. Hn-hn. Either money, or connection. I thought maybe everything had been fixed for him. But when it came to his turn, and the chairman read out the judgement – 'Miguel Domingo – Guilty as charged' – ah, I tell you, I began to wonder.

Silence except for muted lapping of water.

MIGUEL. It beats me. How could one have been so completely without any premonition? I have seen this wall from the outside – I don't know how many times – maybe over a hundred times. We used to go boating from the family house in Akoka; quite often we would take this route. Sometimes we simply came to meet the fishermen in the evenings as they came in with their catch – over there, in that direction. The prisoners would look out from the windows and wave at us. Sometimes we waved back. At least I did, as a child anyway. Maybe I even waved to someone standing against the bars of that very window. There was nothing like the water hyacinth then, so the fish market was a regular event. (*Pause.*) In all those pleasure rides, I never thought I would be looking outwards from this side. The thought never crossed my mind.

Pause. A wry chuckle.

And Tiatin also, who claims to have visions – well, to be fair, she certainly makes some accurate predictions, unnervingly accurate sometimes – but she never foresaw this one, at least she never told me.

EMUKE. You can talk all the grammar wey you want. I done been say am anyway, grammar people no get sense. Chai! Even God no fit approve dat kin' foolishness. My own condition dey pain me too, I confess. But as I say before, me and Detiba we no get choice. Dem refuse us bail, hold us inside twenty-four hour daily lock-up for this cell . . .

MIGUEL. I suppose we can't even enjoy that occasional distraction now. The hyacinths must have stopped the motor-boats.

EMUKE (*hisses*). The man wan' pretend say 'e no hear me.

DETIBA. They've made life miserable for everyone. You can't imagine how it has affected prison life, Mr Domingo. Before, the canoes with outboard motors would come right up to the walls and attend to business. Every morning, very early. Prisoners would lower messages and money, then haul up their own mail, or whatever they'd ordered. The prison officials knew about it but they turned a blind eye. It made life easier – something to look forward to. Those facing the canal acted as go-betweens for the others. But, during the ten months we've been here, the weeds finally gained the upper hand. First they fouled up the propellers, so the boats took to paddles. Then even the paddles couldn't fight the weeds. For over three months now, not one canoe has been able to find its way anywhere close to the wall.

EMUKE. What about the Ijaw boy wey drown?

DETIBA. Oh yes, that was a horrible day. Can you imagine, we actually watched someone drown one morning. No way to help. Just watched his legs get more and more entangled in those slimy long roots. It was as if some hidden monster kept dragging him down.

MIGUEL. You saw him?

DETIBA. Everybody watched, all the inmates on the water side of the prison. You see, after the boats gave up, he and two, maybe three other strong swimmers would find a passage through the hyacinths with waterproof packs and carry on business. The scale was reduced of course but it was still better than this present nothing. Then the other swimmers also gave up, leaving only him. Until one Sunday morning . . .

Rapid footsteps across the cell.

MIGUEL. This window? You watched him through this window?

EMUKE. Which other window you see inside here?

Silence.

MIGUEL (*softly*). I have never seen death at close quarters, not even on the roads with all their carnage.

Silence.

EMUKE. Wetin make you come back Mister? I wan' know. I no sabbe dat kin' ting at all. Your family get money, dem get property, dem get plenty influence. You fit dey Russia or Australia by now and nobody fit catch up. Wetin happen? I just wan' know. You bribe tribunal and then dey disappoint you? For my home town, people for say na your enemy take medicine spoil your mind for dat kin' ting to happen.

DETIBA. Let the man have his peace, Emuke. He'll tell us in his own time. After all we'll have plenty of it on our hands. (*Bitter laugh.*) A whole life sentence of it.

EMUKE. That's if they no fire us tomorrow. These soja people, I no trust them. They fit wake up tomorrow and say – line up everybody awaiting execution. Fire them one time!

DETIBA. No-o-o. Even when sentence was passed, I was already thinking how many years we would actually spend in gaol. I agree with that Superintendent.

EMUKE. Wetin you dey talk? You no take your own ear hear sentence? Hey, Mr Domingo, wetin you think?

MIGUEL. What?

EMUKE (*irritably*). The man mind done travel! Detiba and I dey argue about this sentence. You think na 'shakara' den make? You tink dey no go put us for firing squad?

MIGUEL. I'm afraid they won't, that's what I'm afraid of. Because I can't think of passing twenty years or more behind these walls. Behind any walls. But I fear they will commute it to life. It's obvious.

EMUKE. We go see. All I know is that this na wicked country to do something like this. We know some country wey, if you steal, they cut off your hand. But everybody know that in advance. So if you steal, na your choice. Every crime get in proper punishment. But if wait until man commit crime, then you come change the punishment, dat one na foul. Na proper foul. I no know any other country wey dat kin' ting dey happen.

DETIBA. I agree. It's like football. Or any other game. No one changes rules in the middle of a game. Just imagine, half-way through a football game, the referee says the rules have changed. One side has scored a goal but after half-time, he says it is no longer a goal. Or he says a corner kick which took place ten minutes ago should now be a penalty kick. Can you imagine that? In a mere game it is bad enough, how much more in a matter of life and death.

EMUKE. Only army mind fit think dat kin' ting.

DETIBA. It's their profession. They don't know the difference between life and death. Soja man come, soja man go, finish.

EMUKE. Chineke! Small crime wey carry only seven years before. Abi? No to seven years maximum before?

DETIBA. Until three days ago. Anyway, it's all a game of nerves. And the verdict is still subject to appeal, then the Supreme Military Council takes a final decision.

MIGUEL. Hey, come and take a look. There's a canoe trying to break through the hyacinths.

Scramble of feet towards the window. Distant splashes on lagoon.

DETIBA. Come on, champion, come on!

EMUKE. Na sign, I swear, na sign from heaven.

DETIBA. He's more than half-way through already.

Shouts from the others windows along the wall urging on the lone paddler.

MIGUEL. What he needs is an assistant wielding a giant pair of water shears, maybe five yards long.

DETIBA. He seems to be doing quite well without it. Come on, dig in man, dig in!

EMUKE. 'E go do am. If not today, then tomorrow. The others go join am try if 'e no manage reach us today.

Loud cheers from the entire length of the wall. The cheers slow down. Change of tone from optimism to depression.

DETIBA. He's giving up. He's turning back.

Fade in Yoruba-Cuban music, a ceremonial chant for Yemanja. A man's footsteps descend a wooden staircase, slowing down as it gets closer to the bottom. Stops. A pause.

THE MOTHER (*soft intoning*). Oh Yemanja, sister of the clear waters, fill me with wisdom. Find me the path. Cut through the unseen weeds which enfold my house in a fulsome embrace. Save us from this shame hanging over our heads, protectress of the innocent. Let your luminous waters unroll a carpet of light in the direction I must take. Show me a sign. Point your spangled fins in the direction I must proceed. Unveil yourself before me tonight. Let your eyes be the twin stars locked one on each foot. Rescue this house from shame, from the deep shame . . .

MIGUEL. Tiatin. What are you doing up so late?

Footsteps towards the record player. The music is turned down.

Tiatin. It's Miguel.

Pause.

THE MOTHER. Tell me Miguel, why do you think they gave such a lovely name to this infliction? Seaweed is all it appears to be. Parasite. Useless to humans. It chokes the ports. Imperils navigation. Creates hardship for the fishermen – ask your Uncle Demasia, with his fishing trawlers. He has to berth out at sea. The closest he can come is on the salt-water side of Yemanja's island.

MIGUEL. Did you open this window? Oh! You've even left the mosquito netting wide open – what is the matter?

THE MOTHER. Mind you, under the yellow glow of the night sky, one begins to understand why they're here, from where they came. We humans may have no use for the weeds but the gods . . . come closer. Sometimes I think I can sense a pulse in their very stillness, especially at night.

Footsteps in the direction of the woman's voice. A window is opened wider.

THE MOTHER. What do you see Miguel? Do you feel anything about them?

MIGUEL. Nothing new. And I do have an even better view from my window upstairs. A green baize stretching into the horizon, what else? But you are right. It is an infliction. And the government appears helpless. At least, it's done nothing effective.

THE MOTHER. There is nothing that the government – or anyone – can do. It was sent, and it will be removed when SHE is appeased.

MIGUEL. Oh no! Please, mother!

THE MOTHER. Mother?

MIGUEL. Sorry, Tiatin.

THE MOTHER (*brief chuckle*). You always give yourself away when you disapprove of something I say – or do. Deeply that is, not with anything trivial. When I hear 'Mother' instead of the childhood nickname you gave me, I know I have troubled you.

MIGUEL. No, not really . . .

THE MOTHER. Yes, yes really. But I don't mind, Miguel. I divine the truth and if others do not accept, I am still at peace with what is revealed. But let me ask you something – is this the first time these waters have been blockaded?

MIGUEL. Blockaded? How?

THE MOTHER. Think back, Miguel. Think of the late seventies, at the height of our first grand national madness. Take your mind to the oil boom and all that came in its wake.

MIGUEL (*brief pause*). I can't recall anything. And anyway, I haven't the time. There is a car waiting for me.

THE MOTHER. I know. But you do have the time, I promise you. Surely you remember? The result was not much different then. The scene was different of course. Noisier. Lots of motion. And more colourful, more spectacular. Flags on poles and fairy lights on mastheads stretching into the dark ocean. Every night, the seas lit up for miles. The harbour was one continuous regatta . . .

MIGUEL. Oh, the cement blockade. Good God, what strange recollections you have tonight. I had long forgotten that débâcle. So has the rest of the nation, I am sure.

THE MOTHER. The water hyacinths brought it all back. That is exactly how it was at the time – a sea blockade. Never mind that the – apparent – causes were different, the result is the same.

MIGUEL. Apparent? The difference was not merely 'apparent' Tiatin. This is a natural infliction. In the other case, the regime licensed importation of cement from all corners of the world. And the world obliged. An armada of ships loaded with billions of tons of cement, sealing up the harbours and even extending beyond our territorial waters. Christ, they certainly made us the laughing stock of the world. The treasury was emptied paying demurrage to ship-owners!

THE MOTHER. You did not find the event – planned? Deliberate?

MIGUEL. Oh I know some claimed it was a conspiracy by foreign powers. Plenty of talk about the western powers conspiring to bring the nation to its knees, strangle its economy, etcetera. That was soon debunked. A simple case of greedy operators, a perfect partnership of business and military.

THE MOTHER. Hm. We are agreed on one thing anyway.

The nation was blockaded. As it now is. The army was in power. As it is now.

MIGUEL. Not merely in power. They thought they were the nation.

THE MOTHER. I tell you Miguel, it will prove to have been a thousand times easier to get rid of that fleet of cement-laden ships than it will be to remove these spongy, uninvited guests. Actually they are not unlike the army interlopers. They choke us. Their embrace suffocates the nation. But they are mere mortals, that's the difference. They think they are gods but they are mere men. (*Pause*.) Or lettuce.

MIGUEL. Lettuce, Tiatin?

THE MOTHER. Hasn't it struck you sometimes as you watch them massed on the parade ground? In those olive green fatigues starched and ironed a deadly gloss. That's when they most resemble a field of crisp lettuce. A kind of mutation but still – lettuce.

MIGUEL (*laughing*). Oh Tiatin.

THE MOTHER. But deadly. Poisonous. Nothing I would introduce into a bowl of salad.

MIGUEL. You are impossible tonight.

THE MOTHER. Maybe. But it will be far easier to get rid of this real – though also inedible – lettuce; you'll remind me I said so.

MIGUEL. That's possible. Quite possible. So far it has defeated technicians and scientists – marine biologists and all. They are running around like a rudderless boat, pontificating, doing the old trial and error routine . . . damn! What am I doing getting into a discussion with you over water hyacinths at this time of the night!

THE MOTHER. It isn't just the time of the night, is it?

MIGUEL (*soberly*). No it's not. I have to leave. The car is waiting.

A sigh from THE MOTHER. *She walks across to a chair.*
Sound of chair scraping against the floor.

THE MOTHER. Sit down, Miguel.

MIGUEL. Tiatin . . .

THE MOTHER. Give me fifteen minutes, no, ten. I shall say my piece and then you may leave. Just a small reminder of your family's history, how once it also looked as if we had reached rock bottom.

MIGUEL. You've picked a bad night for family history, Tiatin. The family history is on record, and this son is in one hell of a hurry.

THE MOTHER. We have a name to maintain. Confronted by these barbarians in uniform, that becomes even more important. We have to show them we are from durable stock. We too have fought battles and won. We bear honourable scars.

MIGUEL. I know. But there is more than the family name at stake at this moment. There is the all-important question of my life. No Tiatin, don't say anything. Maybe I am a gambler, like grandfather, but I do not gamble with my life.

THE MOTHER. I am even less of a gambler than you, Miguel. I am also a mother. Your mother. Can you imagine I would gamble with your life?

MIGUEL (*scraping of chair as he rises*). Daybreak mustn't find me in this house. The earlier I leave . . .

THE MOTHER. You don't know when I shall see you again. And you'll be missing next Saturday . . .

MIGUEL. Next Saturday? What about it?

THE MOTHER. It's the Saturday of the Easter weekend, Miguel!

MIGUEL. Our family day? It had escaped my mind.

Pause.

Actually it is more *your* day isn't it? Yemanja's Festival
Day on the island. That's why you picked it.

THE MOTHER. It's the day the Domingo clan reunites
each year – that's what matters. And you'll be missing.

MIGUEL. All right then. Ten minutes, no more.

THE MOTHER. The clock is above my head. You can start
counting after you've turned off that music.

Footsteps towards the player.

MIGUEL. I hate to be the one to silence the praise songs of
Yemanja . . .

THE MOTHER. Her devotee permits it.

MIGUEL. So, I dare.

Click. Music off.

THE MOTHER. Come and sit here, beside me.

MIGUEL. Ten minutes, you promised.

Footsteps across. Chair against the floor.

THE MOTHER. Thank you. (*Pause*.) There is not much
to say. Not now that you have clearly decided. But I must
speak with that other Miguel. Not the one who is so
brilliant, a little rash and impetuous like his great grandfather and his father. Not the sensitive one who will yet
put into his profession all the music which his mother's life
should have been, no, not that Miguel. I want to talk to the
Miguel who is much more like his grandfather.

MIGUEL. So now I am the gambler of the family?

THE MOTHER. That's what the family remembers him
by. But I think of him more as the careless one. Forgetful.
The Domingo who always forgot.

MIGUEL. Forgetful! Grandfather? That's not how I
remember him. He was the least forgetful . . .

THE MOTHER. Forgetful of his roots, Miguel. Forgetful

of himself. Of the name of the Domingos! No Domingo who takes pride in that name, who remembers what that name means in Lagos, would gamble away the family fortune, the family name.

MIGUEL. I know the story Tiatin. The family fortune was rebuilt. That past is forgotten.

THE MOTHER. And the family name which he also gambled away? Must you in your turn toss it away? Oduaiye Domingo sat at dawn at the gambling table. He had lost all his money, then the family plantation, the golf course, the stables, this very house – our ancestral home! Finally there was nothing left to risk – except the name. (*Bitter laugh*.) You have to hand it to your grandfather though. No one else I know of has ever gambled away a name. I mean, to think of that in the dying moments of the game, just before dawn! He tried to gamble off our other estates on the island part of Lagos but his gambling partners knew better. They told him, sorry, all that is already mortgaged, for all we know. He tried one business after another but no one quite knew what the status of the business was, and gamblers are practical, hard-headed people – your grandfather being the exception of course. Finally, with nothing left which anyone would accept, he put his name on the table. There you are he said – Double or quits. The name of the Domingo against all my debts. (*Pause*.) At first they laughed, then the novelty of the idea hit them. So they made him sign a piece of paper, but there was no need. Oduaiye Domingo was a man of his word.

MIGUEL. The Domingos appear to wallow in that reputation, I've noticed. It can be a burden.

THE MOTHER. The man who brought us back – whether as freed slaves or as seeds in his loins established that family code. The family lore is that he flogged his sons with the very whip he used on his horses – if they made the mistake of breaking their word. Even in jest. Your great grandfather burnt the words which still decorate the lintel on the original bungalow – A Domingo – Is – His – Word. It is the first thing you were all taught to read – once you had mastered the alphabet.

MIGUEL. Then great grandson Miguel Domingo hereby re-interprets that lop-sided lesson to suit the circumstances. I gave no one my word.

THE MOTHER. But your bail bond Miguel!

MIGUEL. A legal contract only. If I break it, they keep the money. What more can they demand? This regime changed the rules *after* the bond. The entire agreement has been rendered null and void.

THE MOTHER. I have lit sixty candles to Santa Yemanja. I asked for a sign and I received it. You are in no danger whatsoever. I read your innocence in the serenity of her gaze. She takes the innocent under her protection.

MIGUEL. I wish I shared your faith.

THE MOTHER. But you *are* innocent. Miguel, you *are* innocent?

THE MOTHER. You see? You still ask me that. If even you can still doubt me . . .

THE MOTHER. No, it's you who doubt yourself. When you say, I wish I shared your faith, what does that mean? My faith is in you. I have faith in your innocence, and that means that I see you in the embrace of Yemanja, protectress of the innocent. Nothing, no one can harm you.

MIGUEL. I'm sorry but that is one argument I can never win. Not with you. As for the other one, the name of the Domingos, I prefer not to risk it by presenting myself in court tomorrow. Let them try me *in absentia*.

THE MOTHER. Your family has a stake in this matter Miguel. Your bail was given to the family. But for that

name, the judge would have refused bail. Do you dispute
that?

MIGUEL. Why should I? I know it's true. The other two
standing trial with me have spent over nine months in
prison custody.

THE MOTHER. Then you know it. You know it is not your
affair alone.

MIGUEL. Tiatin, listen please, listen to me very carefully.
Tomorrow . . .

THE MOTHER. We have the best lawyer in the country.
He has never lost a criminal case. The family will spend its
entire fortune if need be. And we have contacts at the very
highest level. Your Uncle Demasia . . .

MIGUEL. I am grateful Tiatin. But listen to me. Just listen
for a moment. No, PLEASE (*Pause.*) Try now and grasp
the difference. (*He speaks with slow emphasis.*) When I
was first arraigned, it was under a civilian government and
the crime I am accused of did not carry a capital forfeit.
Now it is death by firing squad. You heard it yourself
Tiatin.

THE MOTHER. How does that affect you? Your so-called
crime and arrest took place long before the decree. It can
only affect future offenders.

MIGUEL. Did you listen Tiatin? Did you *listen* to that man
as he read out the new decree on television? The one with
the voice of cold slurry swilling through concrete mixers.
The decree affects all those currently standing trial.

THE MOTHER. That was not the way I heard it. And what
if it did anyway? You are innocent. Running away will
however paint you guilty in the eyes of the world. Miguel,
the Domingos do not run. Even your grandfather under-
stood that. He changed his name – yes, he led a wretched
existence till he died but he remained here. Disgraced,
destitute, despised. But he stayed! But you will let these

rootless gangsters chase you out? These – these people without a name?

MIGUEL. Tiatin . . .

THE MOTHER. Look at this quarter. A century ago it was swamp. Nothing but swamp. Not even the water hyacinth thought it worth the trouble of a visitation. Only toads, inedible crabs and mudskippers. A small timberyard was the only sign of life, and a shack with a wooden floor raised on stilts and joined to land by a rickety walkway, where the Cherubim and Seraphim Sect came to dance and pray every evening and on Sundays. Your ancestor roamed the whole of Lagos, found it was the only piece of property he could afford. He bought it and drained it. He turned it into a thriving plantation. The first ever golf course in Lagos was built here, before even the Europeans built the one at Ikoyi. He was fond of golf. Pa Manuel was an exception that way. The other returnees generally took to racing and polo but, he loved golf. So he built that golf course here, just for him and his friends. The Europeans and other aliens used to join him. In those days they were proud to be seen with the Domingos . . .

MIGUEL. Tiatin . . .

THE MOTHER. Oh Miguel, my Miguel, listen! I am reminding my forgetful one of his family history. When those lazy, good-for-nothing Lagosians saw how this fetid, undesired swamp was being transformed, they turned on him. They tried to force him out. He fought them in the courts – right up to the Privy Council in London – and won. Then they tried their strong-arm stuff, hired the scum of the ghettos, thugs and arsonists, brought Igun mercenaries from Badagry to invade our home from the lagoon. In the middle of the night they tried to set the house on fire! Tried to burn us out!

MIGUEL. I know the entire story Tiatin . . .

THE MOTHER. The Domingos do not run, Miguel. Your
ancestors only ran when they were slaves. Then they ran,
and ran, and ran. They took only their gods with them as
they ran from one island in the Caribbean to another. San
Domingo, Haiti, Cuba. Till they were shipped back to
their West African ancestral lands. But the running is over
Miguel, the running is over. Here! On this earth of Sango,
Yemanja, Osun, Ososi! Some of the returnees chose
Abomey, Fernando Po, Douala – some even went further
south to Angola. For your great grandfather, it was Lagos.
When he disembarked he said to himself – the running is
over. Pa Omowale Manuel unwrapped his most treasured
possession, his iron *ose* of Sango and stuck it into the
ground. May Sango's axe strike me dead, he swore, if I
ever allow any mortal to chase me or my offspring off this
land. When this house was built – only a wooden bungalow at the time – his wife built a shrine to her own deity
Yemanja, on this very spot. I have kept the flame of that
goddess alive, and she has never failed the Domingo clan.

MIGUEL. Pa Manuel is dead Tiatin. He died over a century
ago. Before this breed of men were born, these ones who
burst through their mothers' wombs with machine guns
and hand grenades.

THE MOTHER. And what breed of men are they? They
breathe, don't they? They fall sick and die. They struggle
and sicken themselves like children over the confection of
power . . .

MIGUEL. Ah, you've said it. They do things for power that
no one would ever dream of. But enough. Your time is up
Tiatin.

Scrape of chair as MIGUEL *rises.*

We shall talk more of them some other time. Now I must
go.

THE MOTHER (*intense plea*). I know you are safe here
Miguel. You are safe! These men cannot harm you, no.
They dare not touch one hair of your head. I have been
promised.

MIGUEL. Promised? Who by? Someone in government?
In the Army? Someone in the know? In the corridors of
power? Someone right within the very exercise of power?
Or – she? The power which came with the clan from Haiti
and from Cuba and directs the motions of the water
hyacinths?

THE MOTHER. Don't blaspheme Miguel. Rein in your
tongue and do not blaspheme!

MIGUEL. Me? Why should I wish to blaspheme against
something that nourishes you so completely? Indeed, you
could almost say I am sometimes envious. I have nothing I
believe in.

THE MOTHER (*fiercely*). Last Saturday, as with nearly
every Saturday since your arrest, Iyalorisa went into
trance after trance invoking the goddess over you, Miguel.
Oh it has been a double Passion week for my island people
Miguel. We have fasted as never before in Lent, and our
Santa has revealed her benevolent face to us. So do not
ever take that name in vain.

MIGUEL. I do not. You are unjust Tiatin. How many
Saturdays have I risen early just to watch you don your
white robes and blue sash, your face motionless as you lit
one candle after the other in your private shrine, then
walk, almost trance-like to the boathouse. I have followed
and watched you untie the chalk-smeared canoe you use
for no other journey and row yourself to Yemanja's island.
Sure, I stopped accompanying you so many years ago, but
do you think I haven't shared in that peace I know it
brought you? And not I alone. I tell you Tiatin, it is what

compensates for that . . . I don't know – because you are a contradiction, Tiatin, that is the truth. One moment you mount your invisible throne and reign over this house like a relic from some foreign aristocracy, the next you are mounted by a goddess just like any of the other village peasants, market women, fishermen's wives and the rest – wallowing in the chalk and sand of that shrine on the island. If I hadn't seen it with my own eyes, I would never have believed it.

Pause.

Yet, when you return from it all, it's as if you bring back with you the flesh of that greeting – Salaam aleikum. A real peace descends on the house, a rare texture of peace you could touch with your hands.

THE MOTHER (*a brief pause, then she sighs*). Yemanja knows our hearts and minds. She is kind, but just.

MIGUEL. It is not your goddess who has pronounced a threat on my life. It is not any maid or mother of the waters but men of studded boots, of whips and batons and guns and mind-numbing propaganda. Why! Even Sango armed with his thunder and lightning would hesitate to take on a sub-machine gun.

THE MOTHER. And is this the first we have seen of them? Is it the last?

MIGUEL. I keep telling you Tiatin, these ones are different. Different! They are out to prove something, I don't know what. But I do not wish to find out – at least, not while I am within their reach. I do not want to be proof of whatever they wish to prove. Tiatin, there is something about these people which robs me of my sleep.

THE MOTHER. And my sleep, Miguel? The sleep of the Domingos, compelled to face the world each day, knowing that one of theirs has fled? Has run off like a coward?

Stamped his guilt on the gates, on the walls of their
ancestors? And your little sister still in college? Your
nephews and nieces. And the rest of the Domingos when
they attempt to take their hard-earned pride of place in
society? Shall we retire from society, lock up our windows
and gates? Shall we change our name like your grandfather
did?

MIGUEL. But my LIFE Tiatin, my life! You want me to
place my life at risk because of family pride? Because of
your place in society? Tiatin, this is a society of short
memories – how often have you said it? How often have
you complained – oh and with such bitterness! – of the
failure of that same society to give the Domingos credit for
moulding the being of Lagos out of swamp and sludge!
Yes, let's say I run away. Give them three months, even
one, and I swear no one will even recall the affair of Miguel
Domingo!

THE MOTHER. And we? You think we also have a short
memory?

MIGUEL. Enough! Enough, Tiatin, I am leaving. Now,
before dawn. I am innocent. But I do not wish to die to
prove it to anyone, not even to the Domingo clan!

MIGUEL's *footsteps going off. Sound of suitcase hitting
the floor. A key is turned in the lock. The door creaks open.*

THE MOTHER. Where will you go?

MIGUEL. It's all arranged. I shall stay with a friend – you
know him, Chime – tonight. Tomorrow he'll drive me
over to the East. Calabar or Port Harcourt. Oron is also
likely – it's full of smugglers – their boats are fast and they
know the creeks. From there by boat to Fernando Po . . .
if the hyacinths have not yet taken over that coastline. In
which case we'll head for Obudu Ranch and cross over
from there to the Cameroon.

THE MOTHER. Fernando Po? You've been in touch with
Cousin Vicky?

MIGUEL. Naturally I shall look up our relations but I
shan't be staying with them. I made friends when we went
there on holiday in 'eighty. I've kept in touch with them.

THE MOTHER. Well, thank Yemanja for small mercies.
At least Macias is no longer in charge. That place had
become a cemetery for our countrymen, especially the
labour migrants from the East.

MIGUEL. I wouldn't have dreamt of sharing the same
borders with that madman, not even for a day. No, the
situation is much better now. Even for business. These
friends of mine – they're easterners – they're really making
their millions, and they've offered me a partnership.

THE MOTHER. Doing what?

MIGUEL. There you go again . . .

THE MOTHER. I have every reason to be cautious. It was
also 'friends' who got you, us, into this present mess.

MIGUEL. Believe me Tiatin, their business is completely
legitimate. Totally and lucratively! (*Laughs*.) You should
see their factories – plastic and other synthetic products.
Their other line is refining natural oils for export. I have
personally inspected their export ledger. I mean, in hard
currency.

Pause.

THE MOTHER. We shall all pray for you. Go with God –
whichever one you believe in.

MIGUEL. Oh Tiatin . . .

Rapid strides across the room. Sighs as they hug each other.

THE MOTHER. Yemanja will protect you. Go to Oron.
You'll find no shortage of boats from there.

MIGUEL. I love you, Tiatin.

THE MOTHER. You are my favourite, you know that. A mother should avoid favourites but I cannot help it. Your siblings knew it even as children, to my eternal embarrassment. But you are so much like the image I retain of Omowale Manuel. Stubborn, strong willed even when he knew he was wrong.

MIGUEL. Now she wants to start another argument.

THE MOTHER. No. Go. But, wait Miguel. It's so late. You know the streets are not safe at this hour.

MIGUEL. My friend has been waiting outside while we argued.

THE MOTHER. Oh Miguel, how could you! Why didn't you tell me? I thought it was your driver.

MIGUEL. You forget I wasn't expecting to find you downstairs. And then we got talking. He doesn't mind.

THE MOTHER. Where does he live? How far do you have to go at this time?

MIGUEL. Ikorodu Road. By six in the morning we are through the toll gates. By the time the Tribunal issues a bench-warrant, I'll be over the border.

Pause.

THE MOTHER. Hm. You know what I think is a better idea? The Tribunal sits at ten, not so?

MIGUEL. When it starts on time, yes.

THE MOTHER. The first flights out of Ikeja begin at half-past five. It's hardly fifteen minutes to the airport from here, so why don't you stay the night instead and leave here by four thirty? You can take your choice – Calabar or Port Harcourt – there are at least three flights heading east. By seven at the latest you'll be in . . .

MIGUEL. We need to stay mobile throughout, I must have a car at my disposal . . .

THE MOTHER. Then head for Port Harcourt. My sister

still runs the Palmeria Hotel. She has any number of cars at her beck and call. We can call her right now, yes, that's a good idea.

MIGUEL. Chime has gone to all this trouble . . . no, it's not fair. And it means he would have to drive home by himself.

THE MOTHER. What are we doing with all the guest rooms – invite him to stay the night. I'll prepare a late supper and we'll telephone Matilda.

MIGUEL. There is one more factor you are over-looking . . .

THE MOTHER. What else is there?

MIGUEL. Our famous National Airline – somewhat unpredictable, wouldn't you agree? We could get to the Airport tomorrow and find that all flights have been cancelled. Then what?

THE MOTHER. What a pessimist you are. Everyone knows that the first flights always take off, and on time. At dawn it's quite a display, they take off almost in formation, unleashing themselves like hungry dogs against all points of the compass. Oh come on Miguel, you have remarked it yourself hundreds of times . . .

MIGUEL. Hm.

THE MOTHER. There is no 'hm' about it. And anyway, if you lose your flight, you can fall back on your original plan. You lose nothing. Agreed? Go and bring in your accomplice. I'll put together one of those night specials you're so fond of.

MIGUEL. All right. I'll call Chime.

He takes a few steps. Stops.

You know Tiatin, you really are amazing. One moment you invoke ancestral ghosts to keep me from fleeing, the next you're actively aiding and abetting . . .

THE MOTHER. Be quiet. You understand nothing. Just bring in your poor abandoned friend so we can all get some sleep before morning.

MIGUEL *chuckles. Footsteps in the direction of the door. Fade in music. Out.*

Back in the prison cell. Fade in MIGUEL *speaking.*

MIGUEL. You know the strangest thing . . . by the time we had finished supper, I was feeling quite secure. Not just cosy with home comforts and all that. Simply secure. In that living-room with its high wooden ceiling, Chime and I relaxed on over-stuffed cushions, sipping sherry sent by our cousins in Fernando Po . . . all the menace I had felt began to vanish. The regime faded into nothing – cheap, cardboard terrors, nothing more. You won't understand unless you knew the house . . .

DETIBA. Is that what happened? You fed well? You felt good? You woke up in your family bed and decided to tempt fate?

Pause.

MIGUEL. I wish it were that simple. It would be easier if I could console myself with the thought that it served me right. But what I felt at night was quite different from what I felt in the morning. True enough, before falling asleep, I kept asking myself – why have I been in such a panic? I was granted bail. My sureties are highly influential figures in society. We have relations even in the military hierarchy, quite high up – a Colonel in fact. I was confident that if I walked into court the following morning, self-assured, ready to clear my name, things would simply take their normal course. The case could go on and on and of course I would return home at the end of each hearing. A verdict of guilty? The possibility of that had vanished completely. Was I not a Domingo?

EMUKE. Sometime, dis ting na fate. Man can't escape his destiny.

MIGUEL. When the prosecution opened the session by applying to withdraw my bail, even before the witness resumed his testimony . . . then, that banished shiver of doubt returned . . .

DETIBA. Me too. That's when I said to myself, this is no longer routine business.

EMUKE. Well, na you give them chance. You chop belleful, you drink, your sense fall asleep. Instead make you go far far as you done plan, you take your own legs walka inside military tribunal wey don change rule for middle of football game.

MIGUEL. No, I did not walk into court of my own free will. (*Quietly.*) I did not.

Pause.

DETIBA. What are you trying to say? We watched you enter, surrounded by your lawyers. They were chatting and laughing with all the confidence in the world. In fact I'll tell you, I felt bitter and resentful. I thought to myself, that's what money and influence can do. We are certain to be convicted but that one will go free.

MIGUEL. No, I did not walk in because I wanted to. I was trying to tell you, or maybe trying to explain something to myself. You see, when my alarm went off, I jumped up a different Miguel from the one who went to sleep – (*Bitter laugh.*) – as our friend said – on a full belly. Oh yes, I did go to the airport as planned . . .

Airport sounds. Jet engines warming up in the background, roar at full throttle, fading off. The somewhat muted motions of an airport stirring itself awake.

ANNOUNCER. This is to announce the departure of Flight 370 to Yola via Enugu. Intending passengers with boarding passes are invited to proceed to Gate 11 for immediate . . .

A loud click as the microphone is switched off. A clipped military voice takes over.

MILITARY VOICE. A nation without discipline is a nation without a future. The bane of our nation has always been indiscipline. This cancer must be rooted out. Were you at your desk on the dot of the hour for the resumption of duty? Do you put in a full day's work for a full day's pay? Is your favourite pastime malingering? Is your office a private reception room for your friends and relations? Are you the kind of employee who is never on seat? All these symptoms of indiscipline must be rooted out. Monitor your fellow worker. Report any sign of indiscipline to your local BAI. Support the Brigade Against Indiscipline. Long live our glorious Fatherland. (*Click.*)

ANNOUNCER. . . . for passengers on Flight 286 to Kaduna. This flight will now leave from Gate 17 . . . Repeat: Flight 286 to Kaduna will now . . .

STAFF (*shouting over the last words*). Will you please stand in line. Stand in line! It's people like you being preached to by BAI.

PASSENGER. BAI-BAI, Madam. (*Laughter.*)

WOMAN. I want my boarding pass . . .

STAFF. Madam, you can see I am still busy checking in this passenger.

WOMAN. Then give me back my ticket.

STAFF. Which one is it? I have several tickets here . . .

WOMAN. Why? That is how everything gets confused. Why don't you treat one ticket at a time? You too should take lesson from the Brigade . . .

STAFF. Don't teach me my job . . .

ANNOUNCER. Last call for Flight 307 to Abuja and Minna boarding at Gate 15. Final call for Flight 307. All passengers with boarding passes should proceed direct to Gate 15. Final call for Flight 307.

Fade in CHIME's *voice. Sliding doors opening and closing. Both men,* CHIME *and* MIGUEL, *walking rapidly. General airport activity.*

CHIME. Of course I'm coming with you. I am going to deliver you personally to my business partners in Fernando Po.

MIGUEL. Seriously Chime there's no need. I know this auntie of mine very well. She is most capable. If there is an emergency she will simply hole me up in her hotel and I tell you, all the Security Units can search that place from top to bottom, she won't let them find me.

CHIME. Just the same, I'm coming. You stay right here while I get the tickets.

MIGUEL. You just want a night out in the Garden City, that's all.

CHIME. Sure. It's a long time I've tasted the night pleasures of Port Harcourt.

MIGUEL. En-hen, that's better. I'll go over to the newsstand and see what . . .

MILITARY VOICE. A corrupt nation is a nation without a future. Smuggling is economic sabotage. Smuggling is an unpatriotic act, it is next to treason. Nepotism is a form of corruption. Corruption in all forms has been the bane of our nation. Currency trafficking is economic sabotage. It plays into the hands of foreign powers. It is an act of treason and will be treated as such. All forms of corruption must be rooted out. Your loyalty should be to the nation and the nation only. It is father, mother, brother, sister, mentor and friend. The nation is your first family. Be your family's eyes and ears. Keep watch on those nearest to you. Report any act of corruption to your local BAI. Support the Brigade Against Indiscipline. Long live our glorious Fatherland! (*Click.*)

Silence. Then abrupt resumption of airport activities.

MIGUEL. You mean there is no escape from *that* anywhere?

CHIME. It's improved. They've found someone who can actually string some intelligible words together.

MIGUEL. Go and get those tickets, Chime. Let's get me out of here.

CHIME. Where did you say you were going?

MIGUEL. The news-stand. The papers should have arrived.

CHIME. Okay, I'll meet you there. Best buy all the papers you can lay hands on. You know you'll find only yesterday's editions when we get to the East.

Fade in announcement over last speech.

ANNOUNCER. National Airways regret to announce . . .

MIGUEL. Oh no!

ANNOUNCER. . . . a delay on Flight 107 to Kano due to technical reasons.

MIGUEL *lets out a deep sigh of relief.*

A further announcement on this flight will be made shortly.

MIGUEL. Not today please, no, not today. Clear skies all the way to all Eastern Airports, please God, please, whoever, please every single deity Tiatin believes in and I will never never be impatient with her Yemanja again. Lady of the luminous waters, if not for me, then for your faithful one Tiatin, blow away mists and clouds from the skies, reward her fidelity to you . . .

ANNOUNCER. First boarding announcement for Flight 179 to Port Harcourt leaving from Gate 21. Flight 179 to Port Harcourt ready to board from Gate 21. Thank you.

MIGUEL. That's it. That's more like it. Keep the candles burning Tiatin. Don't let even one go out. I can't remember which of them takes care of the skies but please don't ignore him, or her, certainly not today. Tell them to take our wingless Airline under their protective wing . . .

NEWS-VENDOR. Beg your pardon, Sir . . .

MIGUEL. What?

NEWS-VENDOR. I thought you asked for papers.

MIGUEL. Did I? Oh yes, which papers have come in? Give me one of each.

NEWS-VENDOR. Sure. We get *Daily Times* . . . *Punch* . . . *New Nigerian*.

Sound of newspapers being extracted from bundles and slapped down on the counter.

The *Concord* never come in yet . . . aha, here is *Vanguard* . . . Sir? Wey de man? Oga! Mister man! Mister Man! Ah-ah! What kin joke be dis for morning time? Why the man come waste my time so?

Rapid footsteps.

CHIME. Hallo Vendor.

NEWS-VENDOR (*half-heartedly*). Good morning.

CHIME. Ah-ah. Hope no problem.

NEWS-VENDOR. No-o, nothing. Is just these foolish people who think it is good to waste a man's time early in the morning. One man come here just now, ask for one of each paper. As I am just putting them together he take off.

CHIME. Maybe they called his flight.

NEWS-VENDOR. Haba! 'E for take only one minute to collect in papers and give me my money.

CHIME. Ah well, never mind. Actually I was looking for a friend of mine. I asked him to wait for me here. Rather tall, he was carrying a brief-case. Blue shirt, yellow tie. Has he been here?

NEWS-VENDOR. Ah? He wear glasses?

CHIME. That's right. Rimless.

NEWS-VENDOR. What?

CHIME. Rimless. You know, the kind without a rim. Just glasses.

NEWS-VENDOR. That's the very man. He order one of every paper and then he just disappear. I bend down – so – to take out the bundle of papers from *Punch*. When I stand up again, he just done disappear.

CHIME. What do you mean? He didn't say anything?

Footsteps approaching.

NEWS-VENDOR. Na in I tell you. I see am one time, next moment I no see am again.

Footsteps come to a stop.

CLEANER. Excuse me Sah, you be Mr Chime?

CHIME (*suspicious*). Who are you?

CLEANER. I just be cleaner. Morning shift. I dey clean toilet when one man come inside. 'E beg me make I come call you. 'E give me one Naira, say make I wait for news-vendor if I no find you.

CHIME. Toilet! Which one?

CLEANER. The one downstairs. Stairs wey dey behind Ethiopian Airlines. He say 'e no feel well at all, so 'e run come toilet.

CHIME (*relief in his voice*). Ah, you see Mr News-vendor, that's what happened to him. I'll take the papers – how much?

NEWS-VENDOR. Na two Naira fifty for the five. Tell your friend sorry o. No wonder he disappear like that. Perhaps he feel like he wan' vomit, so 'e run go toilet.

CHIME. Yes, I suppose so. (*Rustle of notes.*) Here you are. Keep the change.

Rapid strides over glazed concrete floor. They pass through echoing passage, rapidly down flight of steps, then another brief passage. Swing doors are pushed open. Abrupt stop.

CHIME. Miguel?

MIGUEL. S-sh. I'm over here.

CHIME. Are you all right?

MIGUEL (*intense whisper*). Over here. Get into the next cubicle. Hurry before someone comes in.

CHIME. What's the matter?

MIGUEL. Get in quickly. There isn't much time.

Rapid steps. Toilet cubicle door is opened, shut and bolted.

CHIME. What's going on? I thought you were ill.

MIGUEL. All is not well Chime. We have to act fast. I saw my man.

CHIME. Who?

MIGUEL. The NSO detective who was detailed to my case. I'm not sure he saw me – I ducked very fast. He was obviously on the watch for somone. He was scanning the lounge like a radar.

CHIME. Oh, he could be on another case. They finished their part of the business ages ago. The Investigation Squad take no further interest. They don't even follow the prosecution once they've finished.

MIGUEL. One can never be sure of anything. Everybody is afraid. They'll all be on the alert. What do you think will go through his mind when he sees me at the airport? And so early in the morning. Anyone can put two and two together. One telephone call – even if he has not been detailed here on my account – and we'll have a welcoming committee on arrival. That's if we get on the flight in the first place.

CHIME. You're right.

MIGUEL. So do we go back to the original plan?

CHIME. We could still get on that flight. I know someone who can drive us directly onto the tarmac – one of the maintenance engineers. He'll take us in his official van.

MIGUEL. Chime, I am *not* going to try to get on that flight. On any flight from here. It would be suicidal. What is my detective doing at the airport? Which of his colleagues will come aboard to check faces? They've been doing spot checks since the coup, remember? Looking for fugitive politicians.

CHIME. Right. Back to the car then. We travel by road.

MILITARY VOICE. No nation survives without vigilance. The price of freedom is eternal vigilance. Report anything unusual. Report anything suspicious. The enemies of our national sovereignty are numerous and tireless. They are both without and within our national borders. Play a role in preserving our sovereign integrity. Do not sell out your Fatherland. Be the watchful eyes of the greater family. Lack of vigilance is brother to lack of discipline. A nation without discipline has no future. Assist your BAI with daily vigilance. Support your Brigade Against Indiscipline. Long live the Fatherland!

Silence.

MIGUEL. When did it start to proliferate to his obscene level?

CHIME. Blow that! Let's think of what we are going to do?

MIGUEL. Oh, but it has everything to do with how we decide to move. Doesn't it give you the feeling of being surrounded? Everywhere you turn – damn it, even in the toilet!

CHIME. Snap out of that mood, Miguel. Let's act!

MIGUEL. Don't worry about me. Actually, I was doing some practical thinking. You see, I don't believe even the roads are safe any more.

CHIME. There is less risk if we leave right away. It's not quite five, do you realise? In another fifteen minutes we can be at the toll-gate. Virtually no traffic.

MIGUEL. And at the toll-gate? At those ubiquitous check points? How soon before an eager cop recognises the face of Miguel Domingo?

CHIME. Well, are we just going to hole up in these cubicles until they find you?

MIGUEL. No. We're leaving now. But I have thought of something else. Much safer. Maybe I should have thought of it sooner – while we were still at home. Never mind, come on. It's time we moved.

Sound of drawn bolts in quick succession. Mild creaks of toilet doors.

CHIME. You can tell me about this master plan on the way. But wait here while I go and see if the coast is clear.

MIGUEL. We'll lose time that way. Every second matters now.

CHIME. How many seconds just to go up and . . . ?

MIGUEL. Let's go together. Don't look right or left, just straight ahead and make for the exit. A flight came in some minutes ago. If our man sees us heading outwards, why shouldn't either of us have been on the flight? Or both.

Swing doors out of the toilet. Up the stairs and on glazed floor, rapid footsteps beneath dialogue. Fade in airport bustle as they walk briskly through the lounge.

I could be rushing back for the trial. You came to meet me at the airport. Or maybe I came to meet you. A new member of my legal team. Or vital defence witness. Maybe both of us just arrived on the flight. The important thing is that we're heading out, not catching a flight. And discussing the celebrated case most animatedly. Most natural thing in the world, don't you agree? Don't look now, but I've just seen my man. Still scanning everyone in the lounge with those mean predatory eyes. I've turned my head to argue intently into your face because he was just swinging his radar in this direction. I'm giving him the back of my head; let him recognise that if he can. Scavengers! Warn me if I seem to be increasing my pace will you? We mustn't appear to be too much in a hurry.

CHIME. No, no, we're doing quite well, Mr Domingo. Just tell me what you'd like me to do or say. And when. Should I gesticulate or something? I feel I'm not contributing.

MIGUEL. A lawyer should also be a good listener. You've been giving me your professional attention. I don't think he's seen me. We're halfway through; another minute and we'll reach the sliding doors and then we head back home again.

CHIME. Where?

MIGUEL. Don't stop Mr Chime. Where else do you expect us to head? If he follows us he'll simply confirm one of our silently transmitted scenarios; the accused dutifully rushing back home for his trial.

CHIME. But home! Yours?

MIGUEL. None other. The boathouse. Only one place remains for me, that's the island village where my mother goes for her Saturday worship. I'll borrow her canoe. It's only some twenty-five minutes paddling – for her, that is. I have done it before in fifteen but that was years ago. I'm sure I can still manage twenty. And if you feel like the exercise . . .

CHIME. Of course I'll come with you.

MIGUEL. Then between us we can eat up that distance in twelve or fifteen. Certainly arrive well before dawn. Uncle Demasia's fishing trawler can pick me up – Tiatin will arrange it. I'll just stay put until she can make the contact. May take a day or two but I'll be safe there. And I don't think they have loudspeakers there screaming the obscenities of the Brigade.

CHIME. Even if they did . . .

MILITARY VOICE. What are the watchwords of our national goal? DISCIPLINE. SELF-RELIANCE. SELF-SUFFICIENCY. VIGILANCE. A nation which bargains away its integrity through indiscipline loses respect in the eyes of the world. A nation which depends on the hand-outs of other nations loses respect in the eyes of the world. A nation which does not produce what it needs to survive loses self-respect. A nation which is slack encourages saboteurs against its very existence. It is the duty of every citizen to . . .

Sliding doors open towards the end of the broadcast, slide shut and cut off the words. The open-air roar of a plane about to take off. Sibilant screech as it taxis towards take-

off. Full take-off roar, fading off into distance. Over vanishing plane, fade in the mournful sound of foghorns, then a gentle lap of waters.

Mix ecstatic section of Yemanja's ceremonial music which later changes to elegaic. About thirty seconds, gradual fading out, leaving the sound of water splashing against the sides of a canoe as two paddles stab into thickly clogged water. Occasionally the paddles drag up seeming debris which splash back dully into the lagoon as if it has been dredged up from an unending tangle. Heavy breathing and even groans betray exertion beyond normal paddling.

CHIME. Dawn is breaking, Miguel.

MIGUEL. Worse than dawn will find us if we remain here.

CHIME. What are we going to do?

MIGUEL. Keep trying. Safety is on the other side of that beach-head. Look, I can actually see the prow of the wreck which has lain there half-submerged for half a century.

CHIME. Is that it? That brown wedge just beyond the jutting?

MIGUEL. That's the one. Tiatin swears it was lured there and wrecked by Yemanja to punish the European sailors for encroaching. Her island is forbidden to strangers.

CHIME. She really does believe in that goddess, doesn't she?

MIGUEL. Believe in it? If she had her way Lagos would be renamed Yemanja.

Huge wallop on the water. Heavy breathing of exertion.

Look, just look at that! It's like digging up a network of roots. We'll never get there, Chime. It's over an hour since . . .

CHIME. Keep trying. The water looks freer ahead. Almost clear in fact. Once we get over this section . . .

MIGUEL. You don't think we should go back? At least while the way back is still open?

CHIME. What are you talking about? Let's give forwards one more try.

MIGUEL (*in between exertions*). I don't understand it. She paddles this thing by herself every Saturday to the island – that's where all the devotees from the neighbouring hamlets gather for worship. Last Saturday, she rowed over in this very canoe. I watched her go and return.

CHIME. It is obvious. She knows the passage. We've missed it.

MIGUEL. Impossible. From the boathouse to the tip of that wreck, it's one straight line. Look behind you and see for yourself. We've cut a straight furrow through the weeds.

CHIME (*pause*). Yes, it is pretty straight. Then what? What does it mean?

MIGUEL. It means the weeds have thickened impassably from this point outwards. We have reached dead-end.

CHIME. Since Saturday? Your mother passed through here this last Saturday?

MIGUEL. Even in normal times, she does not miss the weekly worship. Since my arrest, what do you imagine?

CHIME. I wish we had a helicopter.

MIGUEL. Don't make ludicrous wishes, Chime.

CHIME. What else is there to do?

MIGUEL. Go back.

CHIME. Go back?

MIGUEL. Yes, go back. Before these venomous coils close up behind us.

CHIME. Now who is fantasizing?

MIGUEL. Fantasizing? I am no longer sure of anything

Chime. (*With increasing resignation*.) All I know and see is the sun inching up slowly behind that fist of mangrove. It separates our part of the lagoon from the open seas, and we are in this damned canoe with futile paddles battling a malicious tangle of weeds. For all we know these roots may reach right down to seabed. Any moment now the patrols will emerge – they take this route every day on their way to do battle with smugglers – I don't want them to find us here, marooned among the hyacinths. The journals have made my face familiar even to the blindest reader, and a policeman can always do with promotion.

CHIME. Come on Miguel, there's no need to sound so – despondent.

MIGUEL. I must spare our family the humiliation of being dragged out of one set of parasites by another. We'll turn around.

CHIME. As you wish. There is still time to think of something else.

Strike of paddle against the canoe.

MIGUEL. No, no! What are you trying to do?

CHIME. You said to turn around.

MIGUEL. You want us to get stuck? You can't turn the boat around in this tangle. We turn round and face the other way.

Movements within the canoe as they turn round to face the opposite direction. A cry of alarm from CHIME.

Careful, careful, Chime. Keep your hands on the sides and avoid standing straight up. I don't think I could find the strength to pull you out if you fell overboard.

CHIME. You really are one for exaggerating.

MIGUEL. If I fall in, I won't bother to struggle. I'll simply let the tentacles drag me down to their bed of slime.

*The sound of water rises to huge slashes. Then tone down to
a more rhythmic lapping against a stone wall.*

The prison.

DETIBA. She was waiting up when you returned, you said.
Didn't she do anything?

MIGUEL. Nothing. And she said nothing at all. Her chair
was aligned as if it marked the end of the futile furrow we
had just cut through the hyacinths. So was her gaze. Only
that had travelled much beyond, perhaps it came to rest on
the haven which had eluded us. I stopped by her side,
waited briefly, but she remained as she was, immobile. I
went up to my room to prepare for the trial.

Pause.
A rattle of the cell door.

WARDER. Mr Domingo, the Superintendent wanted you
to see these.

Rustle of newspapers passed through the bars.

There is something in there to cheer you up. Everybody is
speaking up against the sentence.

Newspaper noise as the pages are opened.

EMUKE. Wetin den dey talk? Wetin?

DETIBA. Can't you find it? What page is it?

WARDER. It's right there, bottom of the front page. And
some other condemnations inside. One of them is from the
former Chief Justice of the Federation. I'll come back later
for the papers.

Footsteps going off.

MIGUEL (*reading*). National Bar Association condemns
retroactive laws. The National Bar Association, in a

statement issued at its Apapa Secretariat has condemned the practice of enacting laws to deal with offences committed when such laws did not exist . . .

EMUKE. Wetin former Chief Justice say, na dat one I wan hear. 'E sentence me one time to four years when 'e still be ordinary High Court Judge.

MIGUEL. I'm sure they'll say more or less the same thing.

Newspaper rustle.

Here is one from the Roman Catholic Archbishop. 'No one has a right to take a human life under a law which did not exist at the time of a presumed offence.' Good, I'm glad somebody is actually mentioning the issue of presumption of guilt. If ever there was a clear case of a verdict dictated from above, against the full weight of evidence . . . ah, here's another – it begins to look like a ground swell of protest. Even the editoral – hm, quite courageous. And the National Students Association . . . Amnesty, national chapter – oh yes, I'm sure Amnesty International will take an interest very soon . . . the Traditional Rulers' Council – they are appealing for clemency. (*Throws paper away.*) Clemency!

DETIBA. Keep cool, Mr Domingo.

MIGUEL. Clemency! Is that the issue?

DETIBA. Give me the paper. Does it matter what they call it? They are all saying the same thing, only differently.

MIGUEL. No, it is not the same thing. That is the kind of language that flatters the bestial egos of such a breed of rulers. It makes them feel that the world and every living thing within it is their largesse, from which they dole out crumbs when they are sated. Clemency! Even a retarded child must know that the issue is one of justice.

DETIBA. This would be more to your taste then. I've found the statement of your friend, Emuke.

EMUKE. Wetin 'e talk?

DETIBA (*reading*). 'In his own statement, the former Chief Justice of the Federation, Sir Tolade Akindero warned that if the sentence was carried out, it would amount to judicial murder.' Is that more like it, Mr Domingo?

MIGUEL. Ah, what does it matter anyway? Why do we deceive ourselves? We're living in a lawless time.

DETIBA. Here's one more. The Crusade for National Conscience is organising a continuous vigil outside the prison until the sentence is rescinded.

MIGUEL (*violently*). No!

DETIBA. No? Why not? It all helps to put pressure on the regime.

MIGUEL. Don't you know who they are?

DETIBA. Not much. I've only heard of them once or twice – in the papers.

MIGUEL. They are a religious sect who particularly abhor public executions. And they are rather fanatical in their actions. If they hold that vigil and they're ordered to disperse, they are just as likely to obey peacefully as to disobey – equally peacefully. This regime will not hesitate to open fire on them. I don't want anyone's death on my conscience.

DETIBA. That is really beyond our control, isn't it?

Four or five pairs of boots marching towards the cell as if in formation. They come to a halt outside the cell.

SUPERINTENDENT. Everybody get dressed. Mr Domingo – and you two, same for you. You've all been sent for.

MIGUEL. Who by?

SUPERINTENDENT. We don't know. The order is from the same Security Unit that used to fetch you for interrogation.

DETIBA. Interrogation? Are they re-opening the case? Or the Appeal Court? Is the hearing today?

MIGUEL. Today is a public holiday. The courts are not sitting.

Bustle in the cell as clothes are changed.

SUPERINTENDENT. Well, you may be both right and wrong there. You could be appearing before a Special Panel.

MIGUEL. What?

SUPERINTENDENT. I'm not supposed to tell you this, but we received a secret circular yesterday. All offences in your category, including verdicts delivered by the political tribunal, are no longer subject to review by the Court of Appeal. The Head of State has taken over their functions. My suspicion is that he has set up his own panel – it's the only kind that would sit on a public holiday. I'm only guessing, but I don't see why else they should bother you.

MIGUEL. Will our lawyers be present? Have they been informed?

SUPERINTENDENT. Mr Domingo, I've told you all I know. The usual form for taking you out of prison was brought by Security. My job is simply to hand you over.

MIGUEL. All right, thank you.

EMUKE. I done ready.

DETIBA. Me too.

MIGUEL. Let's go.

Dialogue continues over footsteps through corridors, down flights of stairs until they reach the SUPERINTEND-ENT's *office.*

SUPERINTENDENT. Actually you don't know how lucky you are to be away from the premises today. Another set of armed robbers are going to be executed. The stakes are

already being set up. Prisoners are confined to their cells –
that's the routine – but within an hour the word will go
round on the prison grapevine, and then you'd be amazed
at the change. The quiet is unearthly, something you feel
under your skin.

MIGUEL. They are shot in the prison yard?

SUPERINTENDENT. No, not inside. On the open
grounds outside the prison. It's in public, you know. The
Military are in charge. We never know in advance whose
turn it is – unless they are our own prisoners of course.
They bring them from other prisons directly to the
grounds outside. All we get are instructions to prepare the
stakes for such-and-such o'clock on such a day. Like this
morning. You're lucky to be out of it. Well, here we are.

Door opens into the SUPERINTENDENT's *office. Men
rising to their feet.*

SUPERINTENDENT. Well, gentlemen, all three present
for escort. Please sign the receipt forms.

Scratch of pen on paper.

EMUKE (*whisper*). Dese no be our regular escorts.

DETIBA. They change them all the time.

SUPERINTENDENT. Thank you. Well my friends, good
luck. See you on my evening rounds.

MIGUEL. Thank you.

*Door opens, closes. A short walk by five pairs of feet, two
booted.*

WARDER. Open the gates.

VOICE. You have the exeat?

WARDER. Here.

Brief rustle of paper.

VOICE. Okay. Open.

Bolts are withdrawn. A wooden bar is raised from its rest against the gate. The wooden gate creaks open. Immediately there is noise from a distanced crowd. Audible moans of 'No', 'No', 'No'. It is a helpless, not aggressive 'No'.

MIGUEL. Who are all this crowd? Oh, of course. The Superintendent said there was . . .

DETIBA. I can't believe people still bring their children to watch this kind of thing.

MIGUEL. Must be one of the really notorious gangs. Just look at the crowd! But, Detiba . . .

DETIBA. Yeah?

MIGUEL. This is not the usual bloodthirsty crowd one sees on television. These ones appear – almost plaintive. Sober.

Four pairs of boots advance marching crisply, come to a stop. One pair advances two or three more paces.

OFFICER. Identify yourselves as I call out your names. Kolawole Adetiba.

Gates begin to creak shut.

DETIBA. Ye-e-s?

OFFICER. Augustine Emuke.

EMUKE. Present.

OFFICER. Miguel Domingo.

MIGUEL. I am here.

OFFICER. By virtue of warrant signed by the Head of State and Commander of the Armed Forces . . .

Gates slam shut. Bolts are replaced. A lone pair of boots head in the direction of the SUPERINTENDENT's office, slowly, as if dragging. Door opens.

SUPERINTENDENT. Yes, what is it?
WARDER. Did you know, Sir?
SUPERINTENDENT. Did I know what?

A sudden burst of gun fire.

SUPERINTENDENT. I really must air-condition this office. It's the only thing that will keep out that sound.

Three single pistol shots, one after the other.

Yes, what was your question again?
WARDER. I just wondered if you knew, Sir – the three stakes, who they were for.

Fade in dirge from Yemanja's music.